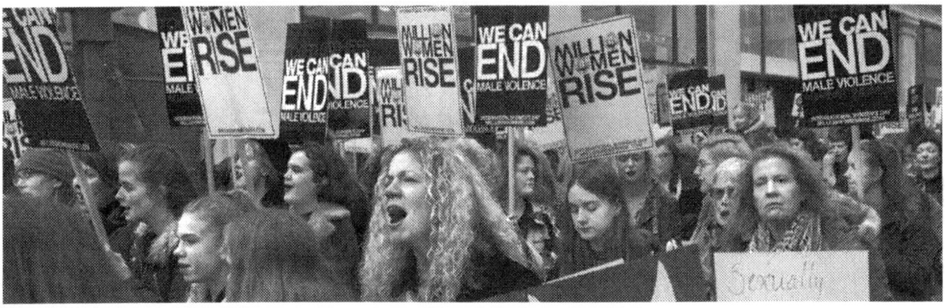
WE CAN END MALE VIOLENCE
MILLION WOMEN RISE
Sexuality

WE CAN
END
MALE VIOLENCE
WE CAN
END
MALE VIOLENCE
MILLION
WOMEN
RISE
TOGETHER
WE CAN
END

Left-Right-Left

A Memoir

WE CAN END MALE VIOLENCE
VALUE ME DON'T VIOLATE ME
ALL THE WOMEN INDEPENDENT THROW YOUR HANDS UP AT ME
I am not FREE while any WOMAN is unfree
WE CAN END MALE VIOLENCE

Left-Right-Left

A Memoir

Teri Darnell

Left-Right-Left: A Memoir is a work of nonfiction.
Some names and identifying details have been changed.

Copyright © 2019 by Teri Darnell, Inc. All rights reserved. This book, *Left-Right-Left: A Memoir* or any portion thereof may not be reproduced or used in any manner whatsoever without the express written permission of the publisher except for the use of brief quotations in a book review.

All photographs courtesy of the Darnell Family Archive.
Copyright © 2019 by Teri Darnell, Inc.

Printed in the United States of America.

Teri Darnell, Author
www.teridarnell.com

Theresa Knoll, Editorial Review

First Edition.

ISBN: 9781795649964

Library of Congress Cataloging-in-Publication has been applied for.

Published by Teri Darnell, Inc.

For Mom and my brother Dan

Contents

Preface	11
Greenup	13
Korea	25
Marriage	29
Migration	41
Trips	62
Fish	94
Beatings	101
Lessons	118
Recession	126
Burg	138
Changes	156
Confusion	171
Epiphany	181
Military	198
Commies	217
Controller	240
Career	248
End	261
Passion	288
Peace	298
Afterword	304
About the Author	307

WE CAN
END
MALE VIOLENCE
MILLION
WOMEN
RISE
WORKING FOR WOMEN,
WORKING AGAINST VIOLENCE

Preface

I'm not special. This memoir could be written by hundreds, thousands, even millions of people around the world who grew up in a dysfunctional home with a war-time veteran and abusive alcoholic father diagnosed with PTSD.

From the Appalachian Mountains to the big cites of Cleveland and Detroit, I describe my parents' journey during The Great Migration to find work in factories then settle on driving a semi-truck back and forth across the United States hauling gas and oil to keep the economy moving while leaving my two brothers and me alone at home for days and weeks at a time. I unveil how my family navigated the deep pot holes and stayed together, for better or worse.

I bring you 'home' to the Appalachian Mountains and tell deeply personal tales of my family's experiences with our relatives, and my dad's appetite for alcohol, women, domestic violence and abuse.

In my stories, I don't attempt to paint a broad-brush stroke about Appalachian people or try to understand the politics of this region. Most of my Appalachian relatives were (for those deceased) and are hardworking, honest, and good people. They would give you the shirt off their backs to help you, but there could be exceptions in anyone's family where outbreaks of jealousy, control, and violence occur that nobody else knows about. It's the family's secret.

I present stories from my experience with the desire to pave the way for new possibilities of understanding and new insights. My stories pose questions that enable different intellectual and emotional responses to the existing challenges and issues of today's society in all parts of the world, not just in the Appalachian Mountains. We are faced with a turbulent socio-political situation in which women must continue to fight for rights that were won long ago. These real-life stories shed light on specific events and voice a desire for equality and to end violence against women and children.

If you've gotten this far, I hope you read the rest. Maybe some of it will surprise you and open your eyes into a world that you may otherwise never experience, one that you can help make better.

1

Greenup

For a long time, Greenup County Kentucky's nickname was "Hangman's Town." Decades of gala like public hangings occurred on the outer edges of town.

When Honorable circuit judge J.W. Moore suddenly became ill, Judge Thomas F. Hazelrigg presided during the trial of the last public hanging in the county in June 1852.

Originally called "Greenupsburg," on execution day hundreds of folks flocked in from surrounding counties on foot, riding horses or mules, and in family filled horse driven wooden wheeled wagons to witness the hangings.

Collectively wearing thousands of pounds of cotton, linen, leather, steel, whalebone, and lace, fashionable gowns and corsets could be seen as silhouettes cascading in the valley. Spectators surrounded the scaffolding awaiting the prisoners to drop and hang during an afternoon church like picnic on the grounds.

Before the grand finale, a double murder occurred on the East Fork creek of Little Sandy, a river that flows into the Ohio River a few miles outside the town of Greenup. Three men were charged with the murder of Reverend Justice Brewer and his no named wife over a dispute about a fence built along the property line.

John Collins was the ring lender of the gang of murderers. He hired brothers Turner and Reuben Clark to do the killings with two other men providing distractions. They snuck onto Brewer's property and created a ruckus in the chicken yard. When the reverend ran outside to investigate the commotion, the Clarks clubbed him to death. Brewer's wife appeared at the crime scene so they killed her to protect their identity from the witness. The twelve men jury trial was concluded in three days with a guilty verdict. Three of the five men received death sentences.

On the day of reckoning, oxen pulled a cart topped with prisoners perched above their coffins. The ox-cart slowly paraded past the salivating crowd as it worked its way to the temporary wooden structure.

Once the ox-cart arrived under the tall structure, prison guards placed black caps over the murder's heads. The fife and drum corps played the death march while guards placed and tightened nooses just below the jaw line. The audience maintained a deathly silence anticipating hearing the snapping of the necks. For the last act, the ox-carts moved forward tightening the rope until the nooses left the bodies dangling in the air for the spectators to admire.

In the gang of five, the Clark brothers received the public hanging; ring leader Collins hung himself in jail prior to the day of the execution. John and Bill Hood were only sentenced to prison but later released to serve as soldiers in the Civil War. One drowned while attempting to ford the Cumberland River, while the other lived to an advanced age.

In Greenup County, the political climate ended public hanging in 1852, but not some Appalachian people's deep-rooted religious convictions in judging right from wrong. My great grandparents Henry Sr. and Hannah Darnell raised their children in Load, Kentucky in the early 1900's by teaching them to live by the Ten Commandments and God's word according to the King's James version of the bible.

Locals knew where you lived in rural parts of the Appalachian Mountains by mentioning where water intersects and flows. Load is where Stockholm creek flows into Little Oak creek and ends at Tygart's creek. Tygart's creek runs into the Ohio River in South Shore, Kentucky just across the river from the closest city of Portsmouth, Ohio.

At one time charcoal was made for use in the iron furnaces in Load, but it's mostly a farming community. Henry Sr. and Hannah owned and operated a large dairy farm on Big White Oak road. They also grew hundreds of acres of tobacco and supplied milk, eggs and cheese to many of the counties surrounding Greenup. Hard farm work occupied their bodies and protestant religion filled their souls.

When Henry Sr. and Hannah weren't working on the farm, the family attended the Eastern Star and Brushart Christian Church in Lloyd, Kentucky. Hannah's God-given role was to be a good wife and mother, housekeeper, and protect morality through the promulgation of Protestant beliefs. The family read the bible at night under oil lamps with their four sons and daughter.

Hannah protested the consumption of alcohol because she knew of husbands who spent their paychecks on liquor, gambling and prostitution. She taught her sons to abstain from alcohol. She promoted family life and responsibility. But her son Henry Jr. was wild and irresponsible despite his Protestant rearing.

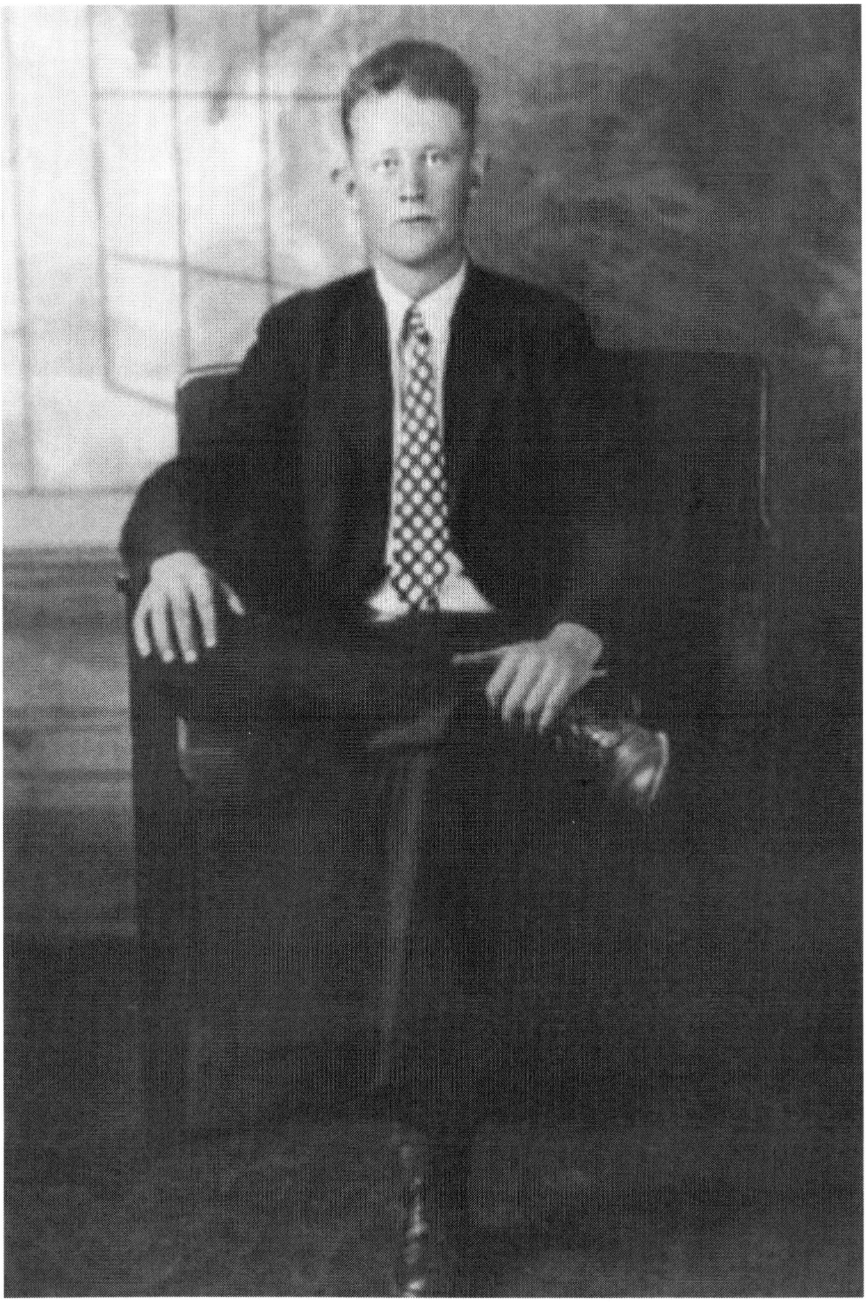

After growing up and leaving home, Henry Jr. became a conductor for Norfolk Railroad. He worked all day and caroused all night. At a young age, he and Roslyn Horner married and birthed two children, Dennis and Carroll Fay. But having a wife and kids didn't give him any incentive to stay home and be a good Christian husband and father. Instead, after work he'd ferry over to Ironton (pronounced "Aarnt'n", Ohio to drink, gamble, and chase women. Henry Jr. was the back sheep in the family.

Ironton boasted of an abundance of iron ore in the late 1800's. Men from the hills of the Appalachian Mountains flocked to the region for work. By the end of the century, the town grew up to be one of the top producers of iron in the world.

Ironton resembled an old saloon town. Mine and iron workers enjoyed the sins and vices available on every corner, especially an abundance of alcohol and prostitution. Thriving Ironton offered miners and iron workers a racetrack, numerous saloons, and brothels to keep them entertained.

It's been widely documented that men who habitually participated in alcohol induced entertainment caused their families to suffer, not just in the Appalachia region but anywhere. Alcoholism and family violence prompted activists to end alcohol manufacturing, sales and distribution. But, ratification of the Eighteenth Amendment in 1919 establishing prohibition led to a lucrative black market for organized crime and corruption.

My ancestors called themselves 'hillbillies.' When self-proclaimed, the name was never used in a derogatory sense but as that of a like-minded community. My ancestors didn't consider themselves poor, 'white trash' or 'bootleggers.' They were hard working Christian people who lived in hard times and off their land, but the men enjoyed their moonshine. During prohibition, they made plenty of it.

By the early 1900's, moonshine became a lucrative business. It was cheaper to make corn moonshine than to transport and sale the corn in others areas because rural farm roads were not well maintained and difficult to access to haul the corn out.

During Henry Jr. time, almost twenty-five years later, he must have celebrated when ratification of the Twenty-first Amendment repealed prohibition. But the Amendment didn't stop a few states from restricting or banning alcohol and Kentucky was one of them. The restriction prompted moonshiners to continue their bootlegging.

Besides being a drinker, Henry Jr. was womanizer with a hot temper. He was known to jump up and fist fighting with men who challenged him in any way. He was tall with a thin muscular body and short wavy red hair. Drinking was his passion, but alcohol turned him mean as a snake when he drank too much.

Henry Jr.'s wife Roselyn had enough of his drinking, gambling, and lack of devotion. She divorced him in 1935, two years after Dennis, my dad, was born. Roselyn was popular with the men because of her beauty and believed she could do better than being married to Henry Jr. When "she done got up n' left" him, she also abandoned her two children (Dad and his sister Carroll Fay). She escaped from her roots in Kentucky to Lansing, Michigan.

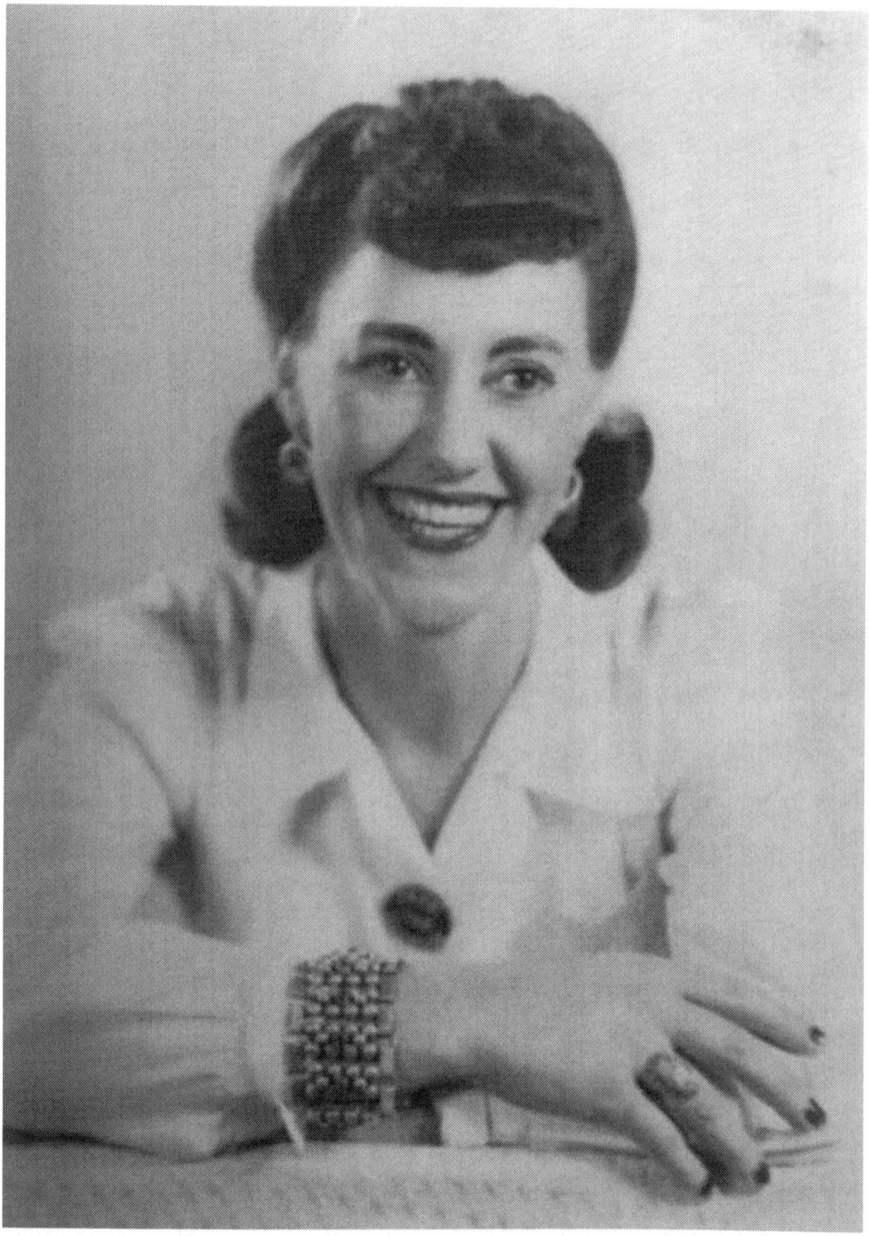

Dad was taken to Henry's parents "to get raised" and Carroll Fay was left with Roselyn's parents in Michigan for her rearing. Hannah spoiled Dad rotten according to his half-sisters Francis and Bernice. Hannah loved and adored little Dennis. But Dad's uncles were jealous of the bond between their mother and him. The uncles, a decade older than Dad, put him up to all kinds of mischief until they left home for jobs to work on the railroad or at one of the steel mills. Because he wasn't their brother, Dad felt like an outsider and continuously tried to impress his uncles with smoking, chewing tobacco, and drinking the moonshine they gave him before he became a teenager.

Dad's strict and religious grandfather tried to enforce discipline on him more than his own sons. He was whipped when caught partaking in the "sinful" behavior his uncles bestowed upon him, though they didn't admit to putting him up to it. "Spare the rod, spoil the child" was the answer to God's prayers for unruly Dennis. The phrase means that if a parent doesn't discipline a misbehaving kid, the kid will become spoiled rotten. According to Proverbs 13:24, "He who spares the rod hates his son, but he who loves him is careful to discipline him." My grandfather believed that the Lord uses severe discipline to reveal our sins. My dad also practiced the same discipline on us, his kids.

In 1940, the fastest way to get the party started for Henry Jr. was by traveling from Greenup across the Ohio River to Ironton by ferry. One late night, Henry Jr. took the last ferry home to Greenup from Ironton after a night on the town. Somebody murdered him on the ferry while crossing the Ohio River. It's suspected that a passenger struck him over the back of the head with a whiskey bottle. He fell off the boat into the murky dark waters of the Ohio River. A couple days later his body was found on the shore miles down the river. Nobody "owned up to doing it" and no witnesses came forth. Some say, he had it comin' for all his sinful behavior.

Aunt Thelma, Dad's half-sister, said her mother Effie told her that the Moment when Henry Jr. drowned the mirror hanging in the hall in their house cracked. The crack that went through the mirror took on the shape of the Ohio River. At the time they didn't know why it cracked, but Thelma's mother Effie heard it. The mirror was hanging on a wall that wasn't ever touched. Aunt Thelma was only six weeks old when her father was murdered but heard the story about the cracked mirror her whole life. When the body was discovered, on shore, Henry Jr.'s wallet was still in his pocket but there wasn't any money inside. He always had a wad of money to show off.

Even though Henry Jr. wasn't around much when Dad was growing up, Dad looked up to him. Dad was seven when his father died and struggled from his loss. His uncle Ellis was eighteen and still lived on the farm when Henry Jr. died. Ellis did his best to give Dad hope.

It was a long cold walk for Dad to get to school. He didn't like going to school and acted out during class in the one-room schoolhouse. Students sat in rows by grade. All the students (younger and older) listened to each lesson and Dad got bored.

Most kids were assigned chores and worked on the family farm before and after school. When two of Dad's uncles left the farm, he was required to help his grandparents. After he reached ninth grade his grandfather asked Dad to quit school and work full-time on the family farm. What Dad really wanted was to get a job at Armco steel mill. People in the region pronounce the steel mill's name as "Arm-a-co". Many Appalachian words and phrases, especially in Eastern Kentucky have an "a" attached – like I'm a-going, or I'm a-coming.

Dad's Uncle Sam was a superintendent at the mill, but Dad wasn't old enough to work there. He accepted his grandfather's offer to plow the fields with a mule, hoe weeds, and set, cultivate, and put up a hundred acres of tobacco for a cut of the crop's profit.

At the end of the season when the tobacco crop was sold, Henry Sr. didn't pay Dad. Instead, he split the profit with his sons. The deception from his grandfather deeply hurt Dad's feelings. According to Dad, his hopes for a future at the steel mill vanished too because his uncles Sam and Jim turned on him and said they wouldn't help him get a job. They wanted him to work the farm so they could get more of the crop's profits. Although mills commonly hired relatives, Dad needed a recommendation from a relative that worked there to get hired. His grandmother couldn't do anything to repair the broken trust. He was ready to leave the farm one way or another.

Years later, Dad got back at his cousin Vernon, who was high up in management at Armco and wouldn't recommend Dad for a job either when he asked. According to Dad, Vernon had lost one leg to 'sugar' (diabetes) and the other one to cancer. Dad went to visit Vernon while he was in the hospital recovering from the second leg amputation.

As the story goes, Dad walked into Vernon's hospital room and said, "Now Vernon, I hope ya don't git in ta any trouble and have ta go ta court."

Vernon said, "Now Dennis, what are you talking about?"

Dad said, "Well Vernon, ya best not git in ta trouble cause ya jus don't have a leg ta stand on!" Dad laughed and laughed like a crazy man until he about pissed his pants.

2

Korea

Dad was determined to make a life of his own outside the Darnell farm. He wanted to get out from under the thumb of his strict grandfather and see the world. He got his wish when the Korean War broke out. He joined the U.S. Navy at age seventeen. He boarded U.S.S. Bristol and fought in the Korean War as a gunman on the destroyer. He served honorably, absolutely loved the Navy, and talked with pride about his military experiences—except for the explosion he endured when his ship was attacked in Korea.

A shell exploded and knocked Dad down a man hole near his big gun station. These guns didn't shoot bullets. The barrels on the guns were over sixty feet long and weighed about two hundred and forty thousand pounds. They fired projectiles (shells) weighing over two thousand pounds and traveled at a maximum speed of over two thousand feet per second. After the explosion, Dad laid unconscious in the bottom of the battle ship. He described the experience by saying that he was "shell shocked." He wouldn't talk anymore about it with me.

While Dad was bombing Korea, his grandfather died in November 1952 at age eighty. Hannah wanted Dad to come home and help her run the farm. Instead, he wanted to make the Navy a career, but was forced out when the war ended. The Navy discharged Dad because they didn't need him any longer because the war was over. The troops were sent home.

Dad's mother, father, grandfather, and most of his uncles had abandoned him, and now the military abandoned him too. He had made the service his home. Now, he was homeless. He went back to

Greenup and stayed with his uncle Ellis for a short while living on ten dollars a week unemployment that the Navy provided him. He didn't want anything to do with the farm. Hannah continued to run the farm with hired help until she was no longer physically or mentally able. The farm was sold and the profits spit between the living uncles. Dad didn't get a red cent for his deceased father's share of the farm.

Dad suffered mightily after the war. Korea changed his life forever. He didn't want to talk about it, but he lived it when he closed his eyes at night. It's normal to have trouble sleeping after a traumatic event, and many people begin to recover after a few weeks or months, but not Dad. He didn't have the fortitude to be mentally tough. He adopted a bad boy image to hide his fears and insecurities and turned to alcohol as a coping mechanism.

After decades of mental struggles, Dad tried to claim Post Traumatic Stress Disorder (PTSD) through the Veteran's Administration (VA), but there was no record that described an enemy attack or bombing of his ship as he claimed. The VA denied his claim on multiple occasions and after several appeals. If he had been diagnosed with PTSD, he would have received monetary compensation to help him pay counseling. He lived too far from a VA facility to go there for care. The bottom line is nobody will ever know what really happened on the ship that day. Maybe his gun malfunctioned.

Regardless of what actually happened to Dad, he suffered from war nightmares for the rest of his life. He'd jump out of bed in the middle of the night fighting "gooks," while screaming, hollering, sweating, shaking, and punching holes in the wall. In his mid-70's, he threw a TV through the wall during a war-related nightmare. In a homemade effort to contain himself, he mounted a large fisheye hook in the ceiling above his bed and threaded a rope though the eye. The ends of the rope were long enough to tie one around each of his ankles when he got into bed at night. He hoped this homemade concocted effort would prevent him from jumping out of the bed in the middle of the night to fight the "gooks." I don't know how well it worked, but he was determined to stop hurting himself from the nightmares that left deep cuts and bruises on his body.

For years, Dad and Mom slept in separate bedrooms on opposite ends of the house. My brothers and I worried that one night he would get up to fight the "gooks" and kill Mom with his bare hands using the extraordinary strength that stress provides or with the loaded shot gun in his bedroom closet. We told her to lock her bedroom door at night but she kept it open in case Dad fell and hurt himself.

Dad also kept hand guns in the house and another loaded shot gun in the trunk of his car. Like his father, Dad was always ready to fight, provoked or not. He teetered on the edge of exploding anytime, even when he hadn't been drinking. Drinking, especially moonshine or whiskey exacerbated his violence.

3

Marriage

With Dad's dream of working at Armco dead once again, he had to try something else. His home town of Greenup offered little in the way of employment opportunities except in the coal and iron industries as a miner.

After Dad's discharge from the Navy, he took a bus trip to Lansing, Michigan to reconnect with his mother, whom he called Rose. A couple decades had passed since he was abandoned by her. She had never attempted to see him. Dad had no recollection of his mother. It was easy to find her. Relatives in Greenup knew where she lived. He showed up on her door step like a stray cat and knocked on her front door. She opened the door, thought he was a salesman, and slammed the door in his face. He knocked again and hollered that he was her son. She opened it again. That's all Dad told me about his mother.

He didn't spend much time with Rose on that trip or ever again, but the trip did give him a chance to see parts of the northern states through the windows of a Greyhound bus. The trip opened his eyes to new possibilities. It marked the beginning of his desire to migrate from the rural Appalachian Mountains to the north, which offered the potential for prosperity in the form of a factory job. It was the American Dream, and commonly called 'The Great Migration.'

According to Dad, he was determined to show those 'hillbillies' in Greenup what they missed by not hiring him, Dad started making plans to leave his hometown of Greenup again.

My mother (in the previous picture) grandparents, Charley and Emma Greene, were also dairy farmers, though Emma was the one who ran the farm. Charley worked on the railroad with Dad's father Henry Jr. before Henry drowned in the Ohio River. Charley and Emma had a daughter named Lena Greene, my granny. Granny married Oliver Moore and gave birth to five children, with the youngest only a couple months old when Oliver was killed in a motorcycle accident.

After Oliver passed, granny worked full time "beating steel" as a laborer at Armco Steel. She also scrubbed rich people's floors to scrape together enough money to feed five kids. The oldest daughter Dorothy cared for my mom (Carol Moore) and the youngest son while granny worked during the day and square danced at night. The rest of the kids fended for themselves.

Granny's family lived in a one-bedroom clapboard house on a couple acres of land. Oliver's father gave granny the property through a land trust so she could raise the kids and have place to live for the rest of her life after his son died. Granny's parents wouldn't even stop to leave milk and eggs from their farm to help her and ensure the kids had food to eat. She'd see her parents speeding past the front of her house to get to their dairy farm out EK road. Not one lousy egg was left for them to eat.

Behind granny's house, Town Branch ran through the back yard and was full of copperheads. The trickle of water flowing through the back yard was about a foot deep. Granny called it "the branch." The kids played and waded their feet in the branch to cool off in the summer. Granny tried everything to keep the kids out of it. According to granny (in the picture with her brother Earl), many people who lived along the branch dumped their garbage and sewage from their outhouses into it.

A large vegetable garden with a separate corn field supplied all their food. Chickens freely ran around in the yard. When granny wanted chicken for dinner, she'd chase one around the yard, grab ahold of its neck, snap the neck in mid-air, throw it on the tree stump and chop its head off, all in one swift motion.

During the hot and humid summers, granny and the kids picked blackberries up the hill on the other side of the branch to make jam. To get to the blackberries, they had to traverse rocks that were thrown into the branch to make a path for crossing while fending off the rattle snakes and copperheads. It was worth the effort because granny made the best moist blackberry Bundt cake in the world.

The house didn't have running water or indoor plumbing early on. A separate outhouse and washhouse stood out back. The only source of drinkable water on the property was accessed by a red cast iron hand-powered water pump about twenty feet from the back porch. An electric pump extracted water from the well for the wring washer in the washhouse.

Granny dried clothes, even in the dead of snow-filled freezing winters, on a triple clothes line near the washhouse. The clothes froze stiff on the line and were thawed by the wood stove in the house before getting put away. Often granny said, "Poor people have poor ways," meaning that people with little money can be ingenious in making do. Granny was a master of "making do." I didn't ever feel like she was poor. She was smart, witty, and industrious.

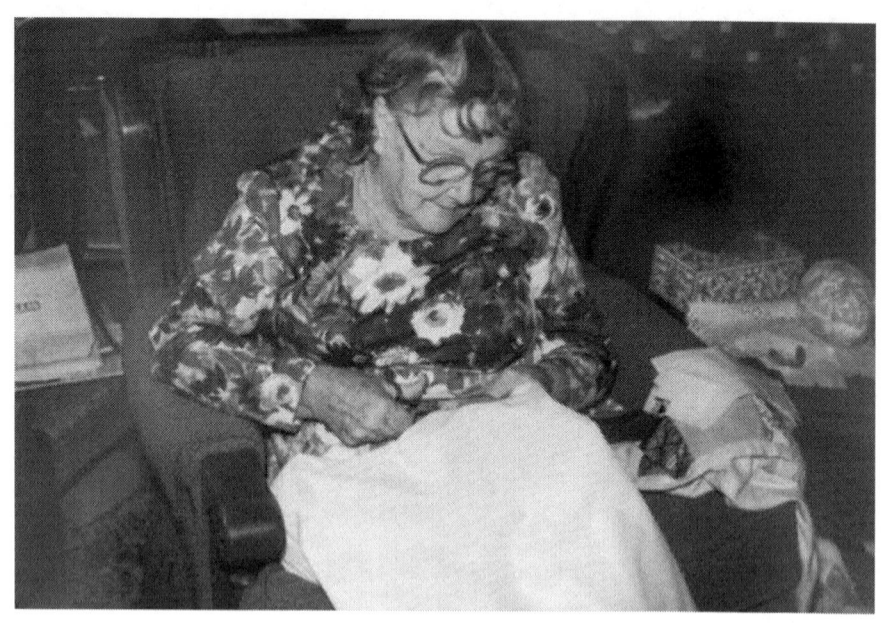

Granny worked hard and provided all that she could for the kids. When not working at Armco Steel or cleaning houses, she gardened, watered, hoed, and picked and canned vegetables. The vegetables canned in Mason jars contained all the food for the family until the next year's crop was cultivated. Every year, Mom's grandfather Charly butchered a pig and packed and stored it in salt inside the washhouse for the family's main meat.

Granny sewed clothes and quilted during the winter and sold extra quilts for cash to "rich people." First, she sewed the colorful top layer, and then added a middle layer of batting. She finished each quilt by attaching a piece of unbleached muslin to the bottom.

Granny bartered to get scraps of fabric from neighbors for the squares or patches needed to make the top of what she called a "nine-patch" pattern quilt. She also purchased used clothes from Mrs. Kratz's second hand store located on the square in Greenup and used the old fabric to make the colorful squares for the quilts.

Each quilt block contained nine squares made up of a solid color and a patterned color arranged to look like a checker board. She'd cut small squares in the fabrics and stitch them together to make the nine squares 'patch.' She'd stack each finished patch in a pile until she had enough to make the top of the quilt.

After enough patches were made to fit the size of the bed, she'd stitch them together by hand to form the top layer. Then she laid the quilt top on the bed, rolled out the batting and spread it on the back of the top layer. Then she measured and cut muslin for the bottom layer. The plain cotton muslin came in a light or heavy weight. Granny chose the weight depending on how thick and warm she wanted the quilt to be.

Granny placed hundreds of stick pins through the top layer, batting, and muslin to hold it all together. She left plenty of pins behind that fell in the couch to stick in your rear end. Then, she stuffed, shoved, and pulled the whole quilt through the sewing machine taking it around and around until it was completely bound together. Finally, she sewed a border around the edge of the quilt to complete the colorful masterpiece.

For fancy quilts that granny sold, like the double wedding ring or bow-tie, she didn't use the sewing machine at all during any of the assembling process. She hand stitched every inch of the quit together. She wrapped herself around and inside the quilt while stitching for days on end in the winter, until it was finished as a labor of love.

1951, when Mom was in ninth grade, granny married a man named Brady that she met while square dancing. Brady was tall, handsome and quiet. When he moved in, he added another bedroom and a bathroom onto the house. The house had a wood burning stove in the living room. Brady added a coal furnace to help heat the new rooms. Eventually, oil replaced the coal, and then gas replaced the oil.

Granny was a lively character and everyone loved her. Not quite five feet high, she was as round as she was tall. She wore her hair short with cat eye glasses while she was young. She called the square dances when she wasn't dancing herself. The 'caller' yells out dance steps and provides entertainment by rhyming words and using rhythms that complemented the names of the dance steps. A call sounded something like:

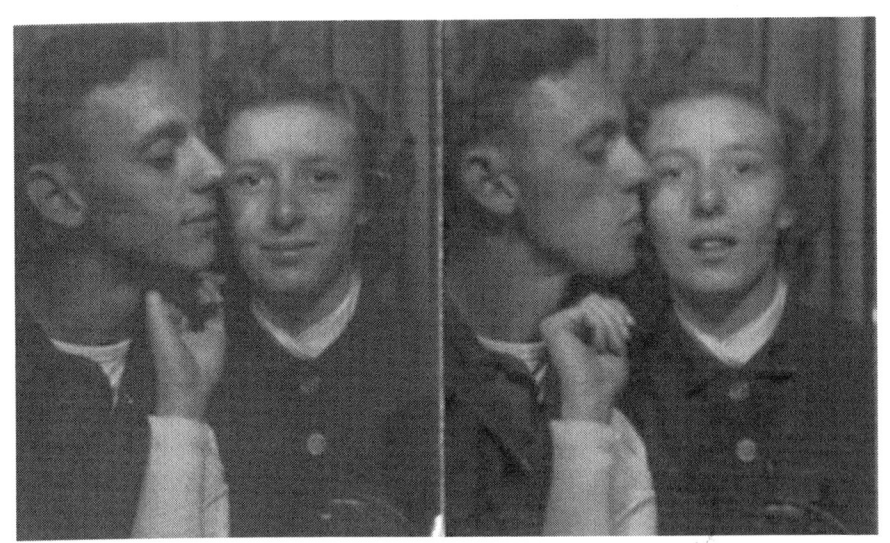

"Allemande left with your left hand, back to the partner for a right and left grand," or "Ace of diamonds, jack of spades, meet your partner and all promenade."

Granny made up her own calls on the fly. Years later, when our family went home to granny's house, I asked her to call dances. We swung around the living room singing, laughing, dancing and twirling. Granny's house sits not too far back from EK road. At night when everything gets quiet, you can hear the eighteen wheelers down shifting and navigating the curves. Truckers avoid weigh station fines by cutting through the country side on EK road.

EK road started as a railroad. When EK Railroad was abandoned, EK road was built and followed much of the railroad line. In 1866, the thirty-six-mile-long tracks of the old EK Railroad were instrumental for economic development in Greenup County. For fifty years the railroad hauled coal, lumber, iron, cattle, mail, and people up and down the Little Sandy River Valley.

Mom was sixteen years old and on crutches when she met Dad. It was the second time she'd been in an unfortunate accident that crippled the bottom of her leg, ankle, and foot. The first time, at age eight, the preacher drove Mom home from church. She rode in the back of his old truck. He stopped in front of granny's house to let her out. EK road was so curvy that made it difficult to see oncoming traffic. When Mom jumped out in the middle of the road, an oncoming car struck her, knocked her down the road then ran over her leg.

Mom laid in bed for almost a year while her leg healed. The country doctor wanted to amputate her leg from the knee down but granny wouldn't have it. So, the doctor pieced it back together the best they could at the time. Mom praises the Lord today that they didn't cut her leg off.

The second accident happened while she was riding on the back of a motorcycle with a young man who wrecked the bike. She was thrown off and injured the same leg. The boys at her high school carried her up and down the stairs so she could get to her classes.

Mom met Dad soon after her motorcycle accident. She was introduced to Dad through his half-sister Bernice. Mom attended Greenup County high school with Bernice. Mom was Senior, a cheerleader, smart and popular.

Mom and Dad "courted" by sitting and talking on granny's back porch through the dead of winter. Granny would holler for Mom to come in the house. She worried that Mom would freeze to death on the back porch or get her leg infected. She also suspected that Dad was plotting Mom's escape. You couldn't get one over on granny. If they went on a date somewhere other than on granny's back porch, Dad had to arrange for a driver to take them to town because he didn't own a car, or anything else. He had recently been discharged from the Navy and was still temporarily living with his uncle Ellis.

Dad and Mom dated for three months and married two days before her seventeenth birthday. They rented an apartment in Greenup for seven dollars a week while Dad tried to find work. That left them with three dollars for everything else they needed during the week.

If you lived in Eastern Kentucky during the 1950's, you worked on the family farm, in the coal mines, at a steel mill, got a job on the railroad, or flocked to big cities by way of Hillbilly Highway in pursuit of the American Dream.

Hillbilly Highway provided the way out of poverty for many residents of the Appalachian Mountains. For those who left, called 'Urban Appalachians' they used whatever means available (bus, car, hitch-hiking, motorcycle) to get to an industrial city like Cleveland or Detroit to begin a new life.

When Dad's ten dollars a week unemployment check ran out from the Navy, he and Mom bought two tickets and boarded a Greyhound bus in Greenup that started up U.S. Highway 23, Hillbilly Highway until they eventually arrived in Cleveland, Ohio with only one small suitcase of clothes and twenty dollars in their pocket. Granny wasn't happy that her daughter left without finishing school. They arrived in Cleveland "without a pot to piss in," according to Dad.

4

Migration

When Dad and Mom got off the bus, they quickly found an apartment building on Saint Clair Avenue in the area of Shaker Heights in Cleveland that needed a manager.

For a free room, Dad performed the maintenance needed at the complex and Mom managed the weekly roomers. Dad looked for work in nearby factories in his spare time. Mom made extra cash typing up handwritten manuscripts. She deciphered the scripts and typed them up neatly to get them ready for book publishing.

Their first baby, Dennis Jr., was born in 1959. He almost starved to death until Mom figured out that her breasts only produced water with little milk. Mom told us, "You kids were raised on carnation milk and kay row syrup. That was what the doctor recommended back then." Until the introduction of Karo corn syrup in 1902, American women took a syrup jug to the grocery store and had it refilled from the grocer's barrels of syrup. Then in the 1930's, Karo corn syrup became a ubiquitous household item after it became famous for its use as the main ingredient for pecan pie filling. Inside Mom's kitchen pantry today there's always an extra full bottle of Karo syrup in addition to the one already opened.

It's a-wonder that any of us kept teeth after growing up with all that corn syrup. For many in the Appalachian Mountains during the 1960's, corn syrup "cured whatever ails ya'uns." Dark corn syrup was once a common home remedy thought to remedy infant constipation. The Mayo Clinic published an article advising to not give Karo syrup to infants for constipation after this wife's tale took hold nationwide.

Dad landed a job as a laborer at Eaton Manufacturing Company just before I was born at the University Hospital in Cleveland. Eaton supported the automobile industry with parts assembled by factory line workers. Prosperity for our new family awaited just around the corner. All it takes is hard work, determination, and initiative to become successful. A good job, nice place to live, money coming in, and a growing family looked just like success. Our family had all the main elements of the American Dream. But what happens when just one thing gets eliminated from the equation? For Dad, the whole dream shattered and went to hell when he lost his manufacturing job.

In 1962, Eaton Manufacturing laid Dad off just before our brother Daniel was born. There was a baby on the way and no medical insurance. Bills stacked up from the pregnancy. Stress mounted for Mom and Dad with kids to take care of and no money coming in.

The grass was always greener on the other side, so Dad moved us to rural Clinton, Michigan and took a job as an over-the-road truck driver. Trucking suited Dad's personality better than working inside a loud factory with repetitious duties. Truck driving offered freedom away from home for days and weeks at a time while he traveled on a lonely highway. It provided a safe haven away from the daily responsibilities of raising three small children. He only had to take care of himself while he was on the road.

Left-Right-Left

In Clinton, we lived within an hour and a half's drive from Dad's mother Rose. She didn't visit us and we didn't go see her. We lived out in the middle of nowhere in farm country, and the nearest neighbor was over a mile away. We didn't have any family, friends, or support. Dad drove a truck all over the United States, came home for a day or two, and took off again, often leaving Mom without any money for food.

I wanted to do everything Dennis Jr. was doing. We used to play War with a couple older boys who lived on the next farm. Danny was too young to play outside with us. Being a girl, the neighbor boys told me that I had to be the nurse to play with them. The farm boys made the rules. There were no such rules at our house. I didn't like their rules one bit. The boys got to be soldiers and sport BB gun rifles. I wanted a gun too. My brothers wouldn't share their guns. They said that girls didn't get to have guns. I was the only girl around so if I wanted to play, I had to play by the boys' rules and be the nurse or be left at home with nobody to play with.

One day while we were playing War and running through the woods, I tripped and fell on a long fat rusty nail that projected out of an old piece of wood. When I fell, the nail went right through the middle of my hand, like the nail that went through the hand of Jesus on the cross, except I screamed bloody murder. Dennis Jr. took my hand and pulled it off the nail while blood squirted everywhere.

He scooped me up and placed me on his mini-bike. He stood up to drive because the seat was too small for both of us. I clung on to him for dear life as he sped down the dirt road for a mile to reach our house. Mom took me to the county doctor to get a painful tetanus shot. That year, I received my first gun, holster, and cowboy hat for Christmas. Those items were the only things on my list to Santa. I wanted to be a soldier, not a nurse. The year before, and the year before that, Santa brought me Barbie dolls to play with, but they piled up in the closet. I wasn't a pretend playing kind of kid. I enjoyed being outside.

On another day playing in the woods with the neighborhood older boys, they forced me to take off all my clothes. They told me that they would kill me if I didn't. I was terrified. I was four or five years old and they were about ten and twice my size. They pushed me down to the ground and took turns lying on top of me trying to hump up and down on my pelvic area with their clothes on.

I was thrown into a wooded area with poison ivy on the ground. I got poison ivy on all parts of my body. When the poison ivy showed up in blisters Mom asked me how I got poison ivy all over my body. She said that I looked like I rolled in it. I couldn't tell her what happened.

The boys told me they would kill me if I told on them. I was too scared to tell then and too horrified about what happened to me. I didn't understand what had happened, just that I had been hurt. I feared for my life. I began to have nightmares of spinning fast, falling through the air, and awakening right before landing on the ground.

I wanted to forget about it but I kept having nightmares. I don't remember the date, month, exact year or even place near our house where the assault occurred. But the memories of being made to take off my clothes, of boys taking turns humping my tiny pelvis, of being threatened with death, and of poison ivy blisters covering my body, including my vagina are vividly etched into my mind forever.

I was beyond miserable for weeks. I was traumatized and shocked about it for years. I didn't know what shame was as a four or five-year-old girl, but in adult terms I felt ashamed for being naked in front of boys. I felt so ashamed that I could never tell a soul about it until now when I have mustered up the courage to write this horrific story.

In Clinton, Mom put up a big garden for our food source and tried to can enough vegetables to get us through the winter. She showed us how to hoe weeds and pick vegetables when they were ripe. However, Mom didn't work in the garden at granny's house because she was busy at school with all her social activities. She left chores to granny

· MAY · 65

and the older kids, and never really learned how to manage a garden to feed her new family.

 Unfortunately, Mom didn't correctly figure out how many vegetables to grow and can to get us through the winter. She told me that one winter we were starving to death because the garden didn't produce enough food to last throughout the winter and she didn't have any money to buy food. She said, "I didn't know when your father would get home again. I called your grandmother Rose and asked to borrow some money for food or if she would bring us food because we were starving to death. Rose said that she couldn't help. She didn't want anything to do with us or your father after he was born."

Our farmer neighbor Ermine rescued us by giving our family food from his land and helping Mom learn how to cultivate the garden for sustainability. We loved Ermine. He was a handsome, strong, and kind man. He took us for rides on his tractor and let us help him in the field. He made it seem like a big fun game while we rode around on the back of the plow and jumped off to pick up rocks. He laughed with us as we squealed when finding a bolder. At the end of the ride, he smiled and handed us a candy bar for helping.

When the pigs were ready to give birth, Ermine came over on his tractor and took my brothers and me to the barn to watch the birth of the precious little piglets. We held them and squealed just like the piglets with delight.

It didn't seem like Dad enjoyed Ermine's company, even though he usually liked most everyone. Later in life I figured out that Dad was extremely jealous of Ermine. Dad wasn't use to Mom getting attention, especially from a man. Dad enjoyed being the one to get all the attention. When around people other than his immediate family, Dad would tell obnoxious colorful jokes, laugh, and tease people that he liked. Ermine got the cold shoulders from Dad. When the two were together, the room was full of tension. Dad didn't usually show this jealous and ugly side of himself to others, just us.

I started getting old enough to witness Dad trying to control Mom. He lashed out when anyone paid attention to her, but only after they left. As I got older, I suspected he moved us way out in the farm country to ensure she didn't make friends but this backfired on him. This new friend Ermine posed a threat.

When Dad came home from one long winter trucking voyage and saw that someone else provided food for us to eat, he became furious. I was six years old and this was my first vivid remembrance of him beating her.

He started by asking her how she got all the food in the house. When she told him that we ran out of food, asked his mother for help, didn't have any money, and asked Ermine for food, he got a crazy look in his eyes. He accused Mom of sleeping with Ermine to get the food.

He began by screaming at her, calling her a whore, telling her she was no good for not planning better and running out of food. He began pushing and slapping her across the face and yanking the hair out of her head. He shoved Mom back into the bedroom. I could hear her screaming for mercy as he beat her with his fists until she fell onto the floor. Then he kicked her body until she couldn't scream anymore. I could hear the kicks in her stomach and chest as she gasped for air. My brothers and I hid in our rooms under our beds for fear he would kill us too. The monster was out of control.

It didn't matter that we didn't have enough food or milk to live on; Dad detested that Mom found a way for us to survive without him. Her punishment was severe for saving us. The next day her face was severely swollen with black eyes and purple bruises on her arms and face. She could hardly walk. She hid the rest of the damage with clothing.

Soon after the friendship-with-Ermine beating, Mom escaped by taking us on a train to granny's house after Dad left for work. She couldn't take the car, because Dad always took our only car to work and let it sit at the truck terminal until he returned. Sometimes Dad allowed Mom to drop him off at the terminal so she could drive the car to shop for groceries while he was away for days or weeks, but not always, in fact, seldom. He didn't want to be inconvenienced. And, a car provides freedom. Prisoners don't get cars or freedom. Mom was Dad's prisoner, and so were we.

A married woman with three young children lacked options for surviving without her man in the early 1960's. Where there's a will, there's a way. Someone hauled Mom and my brothers to the train station. I don't remember who. I was still in shock. Normally it takes five hours to drive from Clinton to Greenup by way of Hillbilly Highway. The train ride lasted a good day and night with several transfers. Mom went back home to Greenup toting three young kids, two holding onto her skirt tail and one attached to her hip, in hopes of finding a way to leave the controlling abuse of Dad.

I believe her intent was to leave him for good. But he came after us. I don't know how he convinced Mom to go back to rural Michigan with him, but I suspect that he promised to never be abusive again. When he arrived at granny's house, he acted like nothing had ever happened. He was his normal joking self in front of our relatives. My brothers and I knew better. Though we didn't talk about it, we were all afraid to leave.

When something was troubling me, granny knew right away. She'd look straight into me and say, "Speak Ass, mouth won't." She wouldn't say it again. She just stood with her hands on her hips and head cocked until I'd fess up. My tongue and stomach would tie up in a knot while my lips quivered and teeth chattered. She didn't let me get away with anything, not even a fearful thought. I'd tell her I was scared. She didn't have to ask any more about it. She'd just wrap me in her arms. She was afraid for us too. I could feel it.

Granny stood outside on the back porch crying as Dad backed the family down the driveway and headed north to Clinton.

Soon after the trip to granny's house we moved to Lincoln Park, Michigan into a small two-bedroom aluminum siding house with an attic big enough for two twin beds for my brothers. Being the only girl, I was fortunate to always have my own bedroom, unlike Mom whose whole six-person family shared one small bedroom.

We had a square house with shrubs under the windows, one tree by the curb, a small front stoop with three steps, silver chained link fences, and a one car garage in the back yard. It was just like the other houses lined up block after block in our suburb just outside of Detroit. A big oak tree next to the garage took up most of the back yard. We'd climb up the tree, swing onto the garage roof and jump off the roof to the ground for fun.

Mom continuously tried to raise our economic and social status. She wanted a better school for us than the tiny country one in Clinton. She needed to get us out of the isolated farming area, get a job, earn income, gain freedom, and ensure we had food on the table. Mom instituted her plan when we arrived in Lincoln Park. She enrolled us in Carr elementary school and started looking for a job.

Mom always put us first on her survival priority list and provided some semblance of structure in our daily living environment. We ate meals at the same time every day. We woke up and went to bed at the

Left-Right-Left

same time too. Mom ran a tight ship. She believed that structure created a stable environment for us when all else went to hell.

The few relatives that visited us in Lincoln Park bragged about what a clean house Mom kept. She proudly showed them around while pointing out the beautiful pieces of crystal that she purchased. They sat and visited in the small formal living room with a couple glass collectables on the coffee table that kids weren't allowed to touch. Mom's brother said that she washed her garbage before she put it in the can. You could eat off her floors. A clean house gave Mom a sense of accomplishment and quieted her nerves.

We ate Captain Crunch or Cocoa Pops cereal for breakfast and the bland school lunch with no bake cookies and warm milk. For dinner we scarfed down a pork chop, hamburger patty or piece of chicken that was almost always served with mashed potatoes and canned corn or occasionally another vegetable out of the can, a Pillsbury biscuit, and a side salad. Dad and my brothers turned the potatoes into a volcano and filled the inside with canned corn and mixed it all together. When they didn't get the hand peeled mash potatoes because Mom snuck in a baked potato instead, the boys including Dad complained. Combining mashed potatoes and canned corn was Dad's idea of a home cooked hillbilly meal. Mom served a special pot roast dinner on Sundays complete with chunks of potatoes, carrots and celery that surrounded the big hunk of red meat.

Mom melted a chuck of butter in a silver pan before placing the biscuits in it to cook. My job was to open the biscuit can and slather the melted butter on the biscuit dough. The combustible contraption scared me to death because it occasionally, without warning, exploded when I barely started to peel off the blue wrapper. When the biscuits exploded in my hand, they would fly through the air and plop somewhere on the kitchen floor. I'd over react from the loud pop like a soldier returning from war hearing gun fire. Mom would say, "Get another can out of the refrigerator."

Granny wasn't afraid of that biscuit can. She'd just slam the can on the corner of the counter, sometimes without peeling the blue wrapper off. Maybe Mom was trying to toughen me up a little by making me peel the wrapper. Or, maybe she was afraid of the can too. The pop sounded like a smack in the face.

Mom made sure everything ran like a fine-tuned clock, but she couldn't predict or control the behavior of Dad no matter how hard she tried. As years progressed, to get anything she wanted without an argument, like new furniture, Mom had to manipulate Dad to make it seem like it was his idea. As long as he thought he was in control, the household ran smoothly. When he felt out of control, someone got beat, usually Mom, for attempting to have a voice, an idea, a thought, a vision, a friend, or an opinion. When he fancied that she had too many ideas and wouldn't back down, Dad tried to break her until she either gave up or got it beaten out of her.

Mom "stood by her man" and didn't try to leave Dad again for a while. Just short of a high school diploma and not being a man, she couldn't earn enough income to provide for us without a husband. Lacking a support system, mentor, neighbor, family, or friend willing to help, Mom's income potential remained limited. Not a single person

Left-Right-Left 57

ever offered to help elevate our family except Ermine. But he was long gone.

Not willing to be homeless with three small kids, Mom suffered physical and mental abuse time and time again to keep a roof over our heads and food on the table. At all cost, she kept our family together and off the street. She became a master manipulator in an attempt to ensure we lived in a nice house, went to a good school and had enough food to eat. That is about as far as the money went. However, nothing she did worked when Dad consumed alcohol. He drove our family down the highway to hell.

"Good time Dennis" turned to the dark side after a few drinks. All his insecurities, adulterous behavior, and pressures to provide for us were all Moms fault in his eyes. He let off steam by smacking and punching Mom around the bedroom and blaming her for all his troubles time and time again.

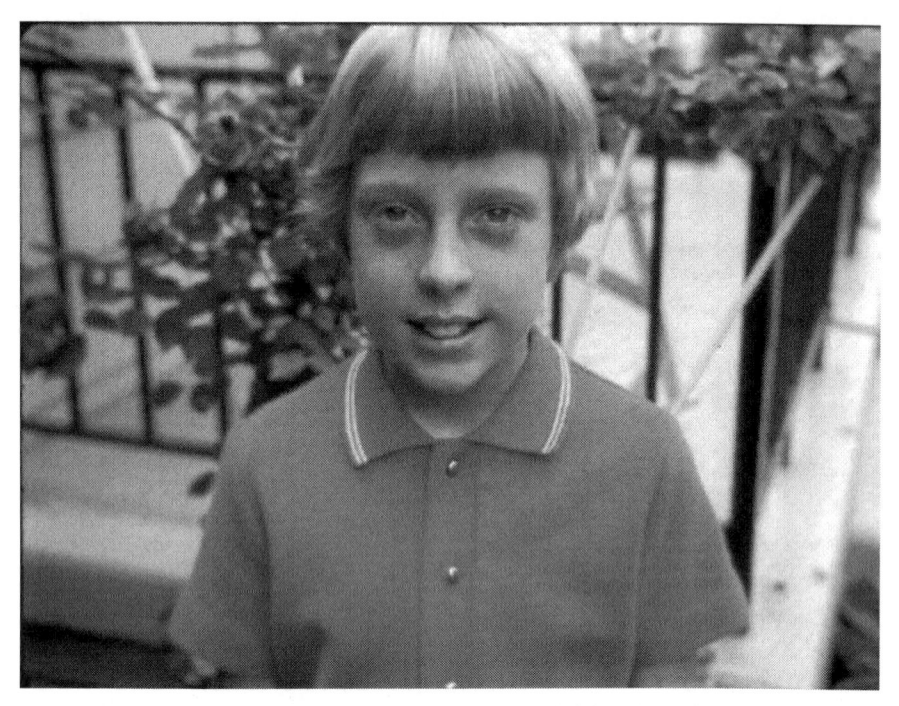

After each beating, he would wake up in the morning and act like nothing ever happened by telling silly jokes and displaying fifth grade boy behavior, like telling us to pull his finger then he'd fart. Or, he'd put his hand under his arm pit and flap it up and down while making farting noises trying to make us laugh. It didn't work. I couldn't wait to leave for school as I watched Mom's slow painful movements, her slumped shoulders, and a bruised beaten face that she would try to hide.

Dennis Jr. failed second grade in the rural Clinton school because he couldn't read. We started second grade together at Carr elementary school in Lincoln Park. Only two blocks away, we walked back and forth to school.

By practicing with my brothers, I became really good at playing marbles. Kids challenged each other to play while walking home from school. On one occasion, I played a girl twice my size and won several of her beautiful pearly marbles and steelies.

On the walk home from school the next day, the girl whose marbles I won waited for me with her posse of friends. She stopped me and demanded that I give back the marbles because she said that I stole them. I didn't concede because I won the marbles fair and square. The bully started punching and kicking me then tore the front of my dress. When I got home, I walked in the kitchen with a bloody torn dress and had to explain to Mom what happened.

Mom asked lots of questions and cleaned me up. She took me to school the next morning. I was forced to tattle tell on the bully. The principal set up a meeting for our parents to work out a peace treaty. I thought the bully was a poor sport because I was a better marble player. The tormentor apologized in front of the principal, everyone looked at me for acceptance, and that was that. I didn't get bullied again.

After getting beat up, my dad and brothers taught me how to fight and stick up for myself even though I didn't believe that hitting anyone would make things better. My brothers and I arm wrestled and I grew stronger. Boys learn how to play fight early in their lives by wrestling around. Physical girl fights rarely occurred. Girls usually fought with words, not with physical force.

My brothers were not allowed to hit me and they didn't try. But we set up arm and leg wrestling matches. I was always a contender to win and didn't give up easily.

If fighting wasn't allowed, what went on behind the closed bedroom door of my parents was confusing to my brothers and me. Why was it acceptable for a husband to beat his wife if "something didn't go to suit him?" We were told not to talk about "this" with anyone, and we didn't, for fear of what would happen to us if we did. We kept our fears inside, even from each other.

Throughout grade school, before I went to sleep, I looked under the bed to make sure monsters weren't hiding and waiting to get me. I was certain they were there, just invisible from the light. Frequently, I woke up from terrifying nightmares that snakes and bugs were crawling all over my body along with other horrid unidentifiable creatures. As I woke up, my bed spun violently. I dripped with sweat. I curled in a ball sick to my stomach.

Before I crawled under the blanket each night, I knelt beside my bed, folded my hands tightly, bowed my head deeply, and prayed to God that my mom and brothers were safe from the devil in our house. Once in bed, I slept in the middle and didn't allow my feet to go over the sides of the mattress because that monster could grab my foot and pull me straight to hell. I laid all my stuffed animals around my body like a wall to protect me from the devil.

Often, I woke hearing punching, slapping, and my mother crying and screaming for mercy. My bedroom wall butted up to theirs. I knew this horrific behavior wasn't right and it terrified the hell out of me. I didn't know what to do or how I could protect anyone so I piled pillows on top of my head and left a small little crack to breathe to dampen the screaming while praying that I wouldn't find Mom dead in the morning and the monster wouldn't come get me next.

In the morning I would wake up to see the bruises beginning to appear on Mom's swollen beaten face and black eyes that she tried to hide while making breakfast. I felt deep sadness in my heart and carried that anguish while walking to school.

I too wore dark circles around my eyes as badges of horror from not sleeping through the violent episodes. Those episodes had no end in sight.

After one traumatic night in third grade, in homeroom after saying the Pledge of Allegiance and singing God Bless America, I asked the teacher privately, "What does justice mean?" and she said, "That all people should be treated fairly, respectfully and with dignity." The teacher told it in a way that I understood.

I didn't tell the teacher that this wasn't being applied to my mom. I asked, "Is God watching over me even though I don't live on a mountain, a prairie, or near the ocean?" The teacher said, "Yes, God watches over you." But I couldn't figure out why we didn't have a sweet home, like in the song I heard every morning. If God knew about the beatings, then why didn't he stop them?

5

Trips

Our family drove to granny's house and also visited great granny Hannah and other relatives each summer. Vacations meant going "home," and home was Greenup, Kentucky, not Lincoln Park, Michigan where we lived. We usually took our only trip of the year home in the summer when school let out. We didn't stay in motels. I didn't know they existed. We piled up in granny's little house.

Dad loaded up the 1967 blue Ford Country Squire station wagon with paneling on the side and opposing side facing rear seats. We fought over the rear seats and scrambled to the back to secure one for the five-hour ride.

This back seat served two purposes. First, Dad couldn't reach us when he swung his arm around to smack anyone for not shutting up after being warned several times. Second, the rear seat was surrounded by windows, so we could act like "heathens" (Dad said this word meant 'uncultured' like barn animals) and feverously pump our fists up and down when we passed a trucker. The pumping of the fist signaled the trucker to blow the air horn. When he did, we laughed, squealed, and got ready for the next semi-truck that we passed on Hillbilly Highway. I'd catch Dad giving an appreciation wave to the trucker as we passed by.

Dad also taught us to count the number of different state license plates on cars during the voyage. We wrote down the state name for any car where the name was different than the state we were currently in and tallied the results. We started tallying by drawing a mini spreadsheet that listed the states in the first column. The second column held the tally marks. Four lines with a slash through the lines added to five. This tallying process made it easier to get the totals and declare a winner of the game. There wasn't a prize for the winner, just the glory of winning.

When Dad got up to speed, he let each of us ride on his lap for a while and steer the car while providing driving instructions. He would say, "Look down the road, not over the hood; look left-right-left before."

Though out my life I've looked left-right-left through intersections of many types like to avoid being side-swiped by people with an opposing agenda.

He was an excellent driving instructor and very patient during the lessons. He taught Mom how to drive an eighteen-wheeler pulling a double trailer.

Our family stopped for food, gas, and bathroom breaks all at the same place, just like Dad did when he drove a semi-truck across the United States. On each trip to grannies, we debated where to eat lunch. Dennis Jr. and Danny teamed up for McDonald's Big Macs. I wanted a Whopper Jr. from Burger King. Dad insisted we stop at a greasy truck stop for liver and onions. He usually won the debate (Mom stayed out of it), so we ordered a hamburger, French fries, and a coke and gagged on the smell of the liver when it arrived at the table.

Hamburger grease made my stomach upset so I would take out the hamburger patty from the bun and squeeze all the grease into a pile of napkins before placing it back in the bun. If I got in trouble for making a mess, I would put the hamburger in my lap, take out the patty, hide it in a napkin and throw it away when I got up from the table to go wash my hands before leaving. We weren't allowed to waste food. Biting into spewing grease from a gray hamburger patty that was rumored to be horse meat didn't settle in my stomach. I took after Mom. I had a nervous stomach. I didn't want to take a chance of asking Dad to stop again to go to the bathroom because he would get mad and wouldn't stop anyway. Truckers were on a mission. Only one stop per trip was permitted. We had to hold it.

When the station wagon needed a fill-up, a man inside the gas station came outside to pump gas into the car. Dad always got out of the car and lifted the hood to check all the fluids. He "shot the shit" with the attendant until the rest of us piled back into the car fighting for the prize rear seats.

One time when Dad got up to speed on Hillbilly Highway after a fill-up, the latch on the hood of the station wagon released. The hood flew open, bent over the windshield, and landed smack dab on the car roof while still attached. Dad couldn't see, swerved to the side of the road and safely landed us on the embankment. Thank God we didn't have a head-on collision or run into a telephone pole.

Dad always carried a tool box in the car. He took out a wrench, detached the hood that was secured by a couple of bolts, slid the hood from the roof, lifted it over his head, and then threw it down the hill in the middle of the divided highway. We knew to behave for the rest of the ride so we stayed quiet until reaching granny's house. The crazy look in Dad's eyes commanded silence. He'd likely have to explain the mishap to relatives who'd laugh at him. Laughing at him wasn't acceptable and usually led to trouble.

During the last leg on Hillbilly Highway, we crossed over the Ohio River on the U.S. Grant Bridge on Chillicothe Street in Portsmouth, Ohio and drove through South Shore, Kentucky. For the last twenty miles to Greenup all that could be seen were hills once full of beautiful trees now stripped to rocks and dirt. The pattern looked like gigantic rock staircases carved out of the hill with bull dozers everywhere on the flat surfaces and giant machines to extract the coal.

Each trip I asked, "Why do they have to cut down all the trees?" The destroyed sections of hills off the highway reminded me of the apocalypse that I learned about in Sunday school. The apocalypse was growing in strength. I felt sadness for all the animals losing their homes and believed that people who stripped the land would go to hell for killing God's creations.

So far, over ten million tons of coal has been extracted out of Greenup County. Beginning in the 1960's, coal fields were increasingly accessed by Mountaintop Removal Mining (MTR), which is a form of surface mining that involves removing a significant portion of a mountain, hill, or ridge.

The coal extraction process involved blasting explosives to expose underlying coal seams. The excess rocks and soil contained toxic materials from the blasts. Those toxins were dumped into nearby valleys and water sources causing permanent loss of critical ecosystems through water pollution and the burial of headwater streams. And, vegetation removal and soil compaction from mining equipment contributed to flooding from storm runoff.

We navigated the curvy road on the last mile to granny's house. I sat in the back dizzy and sick to my stomach. If I complained Dad would holler, "Don't make me stop this car." That meant if I said one more word, he'd stop the car, yank me out of the back seat and set my pants on fire. The "Don't make me stop this car" warning was only given once per trip per kid. We finally arrived. Granny's husband Brady sported muscles on top of muscles. He worked on the railroad and had no problem using a sledge hammer to drive spikes into the rails for the new railroad. His snow-white hair glowed against his deeply tanned skin. He hardly ever said a word, but I could tell that he loved granny.

Brady could build just about anything. After marrying granny, in addition to building a second bedroom on the west side of the house and the only bathroom on the back, he installed plumbing for the kitchen. Before that, in the early days, the family had to use an outhouse. A pipe flowed waste down to the branch where the kids played. Mom later told me that all the houses on EK road dumped their sewage into the branch one way or another. A septic tank was installed years later but not while Mom was growing up.

Granny dumped left over food items that wouldn't burn into the branch, too. She burned trash and anything flammable in a large steel barrel on the bank of the branch. Burning trash at the branch lessened the likelihood of catching the house on fire. Most of the shooting flames landed in the polluted water, so a forest fire was avoided as well. When I asked her about throwing garbage in the branch, she said, "You know too much for one but not enough for two." What I didn't know at the time was that she didn't have the money to purchase and get a septic tank installed. Greenup County didn't have garbage pick-up either, something we took for granted in the city.

Granny kept two buckets under the sink that separated stuff that burned from stuff that didn't. She also kept a pint size Mason jar on the counter. From the cast iron skillet, she poured excess fat left from frying sausage and bacon into the jar "for good measure." She used the lard to make pie crust, fried chicken, and anything else that could use a little extra taste, like throwing a wad of lard into a pot of boiling green beans.

Granny cooked country ham, bacon, eggs, and biscuits every morning. She'd go down to the chicken coop and pull the eggs straight out from under those chickens. The ham was cured in salt and didn't need to be refrigerated, just heated up. She made a breakfast that was supposed to "stick to your ribs" until lunch time.

She made homemade biscuits with flour and lard until Pillsbury invented biscuits that popped out of the can. According to granny, that invention was "better than sliced bread." Every morning she sliced a chunk off the government butter and threw it into a round silver pan to begin melting in the hot oven. She took the pan out when the butter turned light brown. She evenly coated the pan by swirling the liquid butter around. She peeled the thick blue paper covering from the cardboard can. The can looked like a chopped off empty Christmas wrapping paper tube. Granny wacked the can on the corner of the counter with fervor, removed a biscuit, dipped it in the hot butter, flipped it over, placed it in the pan, and finished the rest of the biscuits until they were all slathered in butter and tightly squeezed together. I watched granny's technique carefully because mine needed a lot of work. I admired my strong willed and fun-loving granny while she pranced through the kitchen in her polyester pickle green pants and fuchsia blouse that she sewed from scrap materials.

While the biscuits baked forming a crunchy light brown top, granny scooped out a wad of solid lard from the Mason jar with a U.S. military metal spoon, smacked it into the iron skillet, and heated the lard until the grease started popping all over the stove. Then, she tossed a couple strips of bacon and sausage patties into the hot sparking skillet as grease popped and splattered. She placed the sizzling meat on her plate then fried two eggs in the iron skillet grease until they were cooked medium with the yellow still soft on top for dipping her biscuit in the yolk. She didn't break the yoke when cooking the eggs. She didn't flip the eggs either. She took a spoon full of hot grease from the skillet and poured it over the top of the eggs. She was careful not to break the yolk when the spatula jiggled the sunny side up eggs loose from the sticky skillet. She placed the eggs onto the blue trimmed china plate. Then, she poured part of the hot lard from the skillet into a tea cup so she could lap her biscuits in it. Then she'd smother homemade blackberry jam inside. She made the same delicious breakfast, with slight variations every morning for all of us. She never suffered from high cholesterol.

I slept on the old couch with occasional stick pins poking me in the living room and piled hand-made quilts on top of me for warmth. My brothers spread out sleeping bags on the small living room floor, careful not to knock anything over because there was something in almost every inch of the space, including a lot of breakable porcelain ceramics that granny cooked in the kiln in town then painted by hand.

Left-Right-Left

A furnace with a large cast iron grate was placed in the middle of the house. The air coming from the three by three feet grate heated all rooms. Walking across the grate felt like crossing the fires of hell. The hot sharp-edged grate dug into my soft little feet. The grate connected the living room, kitchen and bathroom with no path around it. When the furnace fired up, it could blast Neil Armstrong to the moon. First, oil sprayed into the combustion chamber at high pressure. Then, an electric spark ignited the oil. Finally, the blower forced hot air up and out the steel grate. The oil continued to burn as the mist sprayed in the air, in the house, and into our lungs.

When I slept on the couch, my head laid next to the grate. The blast blew my hair straight up with each new surge of heat. As I lay there, granny played her 45's on the record player. Bobbie Gentry sang "Ode to Billie Joe" and I felt deep sorrow. I asked why Billy Joe jumped off the Tallahatchie Bridge. Granny said I was too young to know. I was seven.

In 1976, a film was produced from the song's setting. Set in 1953, the 'Ode to Billy Joe' explores the relationship between teenagers Billy Joe McAllister and Bobbie Lee Hartley. One night at a jamboree, Billy Joe got drunk and entered a brothel behind the event and had sex with another man.

After this encounter, Billy Joe disappeared. When he returned, Bobbie Lee pursed a sexual relationship with him. Billy Joe's guilt prevented consummation of their relationship. He told Bobbie Lee that he had sex with a man then he said good bye and jumped off the bridge. The local preacher, who saw them together at the bridge, spread rumors that Billy Joe got Bobbie Lee pregnant out of wedlock and committed suicide because of it. As Bobbie Lee left home over the scandal to catch a bus out of town, she met the man Billy Joe had sex with. As he was about to confess to her father to clear her name, she convinced him that it would forever tarnish Billy Joe's reputation and he could be subject to criminal prosecution. The film ends with the two of them walking off the bridge together.

Little did I know that a single song heard at age seven would stick with me for life. The words penetrated my heart about someone's decision to take their own life.

* * *

Left-Right-Left

Granny enjoyed talking on the phone and keeping up with all the gossip in Greenup County. When seated in her old lazy-boy chair, she'd reach behind her to change the brightness of the room by placing a finger on the touch lamp. We were amazed at this new invention. When granny wasn't in the room, I'd go to the lamp and keep touching it until I was told to stop.

A couple years later, I wanted to use granny's telephone to call my cousin to come over to play. I noticed the holes in the mouth piece were full of an unknown substance that caked the entire bottom half of the receiver. I said, "Granny what's all over your phone?" Granny said, "Now honey, you can't talk on the phone without eating Fritos."

I looked at the mouth piece and my stomach turned upside down. I unscrewed the mouth piece and let it soak for a while in hot soapy water. When the Fritos softened, I took a slew of tooth picks and poked through the mouth piece holes to dislodge the corn, salt, and spit remnants. I scrubbed the rest of the mouth piece with a Brillo Pad until it felt safe to use. She didn't see a thing wrong with it and just laughed.

I also spent hours trying to get the twenty feet of phone cord untangled so the circles would all go in one direction. I finally gave up.

* * *

A widow and survivor with grit, granny was a leader in her community and a role model for me. The members elected her as Secretary and Treasurer of the Plum Grove Homemaker's Society.

In her midlife, granny sold Avon and delivered the goods in a white 1970 Ford Falcon Futura that sported a large orange bobblehead cat in the back window that bounced up and down as she navigated the potholes in the dirt roads that lead her up and down the hollers to get to her backwoods' customers.

When our family visited granny, Avon gifts for everyone were plentiful. We were given soap-on-a-rope, glass antique cars, motorcycles and trucks full of "Wild Country after shave," a snoopy comb and brush set, and plenty of other dust collectors. We couldn't get enough Avon. Granny let us pick out one item each from the Avon catalog during our visits. The treasures awaited our return, and we didn't forget about it. The more Avon we had, the more we wanted, like an addiction. Our family had "more than you could shake a stick at" displayed in our house in the suburbs.

When asked her age, granny would say, "A woman who'd tell her age would tell anything!" When I asked for something that she didn't think I needed or earned, she'd say, "If you wish in one hand and shit in the other, which one do you think weighs the most?" She left it up to me to figure it out. She often told me, "You know too much for one but not enough for two." Apparently, I was a know-it-all and didn't know it! I thought that I knew more than the whole bunch, so what could she possibly be talking about?

* * *

Dennis Jr. and I were always one step away from gittin' a-lickin' or a-whoopin'. When we acted like wild heathens while visiting granny, Dad would give us a-switchin' with the branches of the weeping willow tree in granny's front yard. Getting switched was a laborious process. First, we were warned several times to stop running in and out of the house, quit fighting or arguing, stay out of the branch, be within calling distance, and obey many other rules that imposed restrictions on fun. Dad would sit yelling from his cold steel lawn chair under the fifty-year-old weeping willow tree where we played. When he had finally had enough, he would point at the tree and say tersely, "Go git a switch." We knew this meant trouble.

The tree had enough branches to whoop the entire county's population of heathen kids. It seemed like every house in Kentucky had a big fat weeping willow tree. Every wife in Kentucky must have planted one while their husbands were at war and they were home running the farm to feed the kids. When the soldiers came home, they had endless switches to wear out their unruly and undisciplined kids.

Pliable willow tree twigs sting when they make contact with the skin, so they make great switches. Welts form with each strike, some bloody, some not. Willow branches dry out quickly, so switches can only withstand one good switchin', maybe two. But in the Appalachian Mountains, there is always a good switch around, no worries about a shortage. You can hear a tree weep for you whenever the wind blows. Dennis Jr. and I believed God created weeping willows to inflict bodily harm on us.

After Dad delivered a final warning to stop running in and out of granny's house, he would summon us to stand at attention in front of him by shouting, "Front and center." That meant now, no ifs, ands or buts.

Dad enjoyed whittling sticks, so he always kept a pocket knife in his pants pocket. He would pull out his knife, open the blade and hand it to Dennis Jr. As the oldest child he stood in line first for punishment. I watched while my skinny knees knocked together in fear. Dennis Jr. walked slowly to the God-fearing willow tree.

Dennis Jr. reached high to tug down a limb without stepping on the twigs sweeping the ground. With a quick precise pull, he severed the pliant weapon from the branch with the pocket knife without cutting off his fingers. After inspection, Dad said, "Too fat, go git another." The next one was too long, skinny, dry, or short. Dennis Jr. would stroll back to the tree and carefully select another one until Dad got tired of the game. It took three or four times to pick the perfect switch.

Dennis Jr. and I stood up straight in front of Dad while he took back his knife and stripped away the leaves on the branch. Then, he would cut off a section of the branch that was pliable enough to instill maximum belief in us that he was not afraid to not spare the rod to alter our behavior.

Dad would ask us, "Ya know why yur gittin' a-switchin'?" We would always say, "No." We didn't want to own up to anything that he didn't already know about or we would get it twice as long and hard. We just wanted to get the punishment over with so the layers of red, swollen thrash marks could begin to heal. The thrash marks on our legs were a reminder to obey the rules or get switched again.

Dennis Jr. always took it like a man and I always took it wailing and protesting. After getting the bottom of our legs switched until we showed the first sign of blood, Dad placed the switch by his steel lawn chair to remind us that a-switchin' was only an arm's length away. Dad reminded us to quit acting like heathens or next time we would be knocked into next week.

After getting switched, we would avoid the washhouse where the men parked their metal chairs so they could sit outside and drink moonshine. The more the moonshine flowed, the more frequent the switchin'. Switchin' was an excuse for Dad to get out of the chair, stretch his legs, and exercise the arm that wasn't holding the small jug or Mason jar.

Because willow twigs lose their pliability when dried out, Dad would repeat the same switch-gittin' process each day, unless he wasn't around, which we could usually count on. After a day of hanging around at granny's house he would get bored and hit the road. He'd say he was going to visit his granny, meaning going to Ironton to drink and chase women. We knew he was lying because great granny loved having us visit. Why would he go there without us?

Granny didn't allow any smoking or drinking inside her house. All cigarettes, cigar's, pipes, and any resemblance of alcohol, usually moonshine, were consumed by someone sitting in one of the steel chairs sitting under the willow tree or outside the washhouse ("warsh" house, as granny would say). Back in the day, separate washhouses and outhouses were built outside the main structure. Even though the main house lacked running water, the well supplied the washhouse with water through an underground copper pipe that hooked to the wring washer. The washhouse also stored a steel wash tub where weekly baths occurred, needed or not.

Dad and Brady 'shot the shit,' smoked, whittled, and consumed moonshine at the washhouse from dawn until the lightning bugs came out. We poked holes in empty Mason jar lids that smelled like gasoline with a hammer and a nail so the bugs we caught and placed in the jars could breathe. Now I realized they must have gotten intoxicated in the jars. We twirled through the field lit with glorious creations of God and watched thousands of glowing yellow lights dance through the jet-black sky.

The women stayed in the kitchen sweating from canning, making fudge or cooking blackberry Bundt cakes in the oven until it was time for us to go to bed. Luckily, kids in the kitchen got in the way and were instructed to stay outside and play until baths and bedtime.

Dad went carousing one night and didn't come back, so the next day Dennis Jr. and I decided to explore the inside of the washhouse. We wanted to see how granny's old wringer washer worked. I stuck my fingers in the wringer while checking out the parts. Dennis Jr. turned on the switch. Then all hell broke loose. I started a-screamin' and everyone came a-runnin' out to the washhouse to see what all the commotion was about.

Granny quickly turned off the switch and rolled my hand back out of the wringer. I knew it was time for another switchin' when Dad found out. Instead, nobody told him about the hand wringing and granny put a padlock on the washhouse.

Granny cried the rest of the day. I'm not sure if the cryin' was from the wringin' or Dad's carousin' and staying gone for two days. Granny wasn't happy with any of it. We circled around her yard many times on our mini-bike to keep us entertained. The mini-bike tires wore a path around the house and yard. She cried about that too. Granny was a-cryin' a lot that visit.

The biggest highlight of going to Greenup was having so many cousins to play with. Seven of my first cousins practically lived next door to granny. We crossed the branch and traveled through a field to play at their house. The kids were all thicker than thieves and played hard outside until it was time to eat or take turns hand cranking the homemade ice cream maker.

When we visited relatives, we always met up at the Darnell cemetery located deep down a holler to get our pictures taken with those long gone. Our families posed together for pictures in front of each headstone on every visit. Strict rules were enforced to not to run in the cemetery and step on our loved ones. We managed to behave ourselves and not get switched in front of our ancestors.

On our way to the cemetery we'd stop at a country store to get bunches of plastic flowers, enough to go around for each grave site. Only one store existed within miles that carried plastic flowers in the colors that Mom liked. She'd get the same purple and white ones every

Left-Right-Left 81

time we'd visit the cemetery so the new and the old would blend in together. The new plastic ones freshened up the old dirty ones that stayed in the ground, according to Mom. Eventually, they all looked dirty again – just more of them.

Mom always purchased a couple cotton mops to take back home while at the country store. "Nobody makes cotton mops like they do in Kentucky," according to Mom. She said, "the ones at home have polyester in 'em and don't warsh-up good."

Dressed in our Sunday best clothes, we'd hike up grassy hills, climb over large rocks, and tramp through tall weeds to get to the resting places of generations before us, collecting chigger bites along the way. When we finally made it to the graves, we would stand behind the headstone so Dad could take our picture with the deceased. He let me take pictures with his camera too.

Some families have "picnics on the grounds" at the church for reunions. We unfolded and circled our colorful aluminum lawn chairs around headstones and ate a picnic basket full of bologna sandwiches for lunch.

Sadly, as of this writing in the year 2018, seven out of the eighteen people in this picture have had passed to join the loved ones, including four of the kids.

* * *

I didn't like pools since I had almost drowned at an indoor public pool in Lincoln Park. Mom dropped us off at the recreation center on Saturday mornings for an hour so she could get her shopping done. I hadn't yet learned to swim well. Dennis Jr. and I loved to jump off the diving board. Kids weren't allowed to jump off the boards during the hour swimming session unless they could prove that they could swim from the deep end of the pool to the shallow end. To begin the session, kids lined up at the deep end of the pool. When the lifeguard blew the whistle, we jumped in and swam to the shallow end. Since I couldn't swim, I would jump in near the side of the pool by the ladder, then doggy paddle to the shallow end. This way I could occasionally hold onto the edge when I got tired.

On that day I almost drowned, the whistle blew and all the kids jumped off the ledge in the deep end. I jumped in, too, and a big fat kid jumped on top of me. I sank to the bottom. I don't remember what happened next. I woke up on a stretcher with an oxygen mask strapped to my face looking at a big fat kid crying thinking that he killed me. There was a lot of commotion going on in the room until my mom arrived and took us home.

That was our last trip to the pool. After that I was deathly afraid of water. My aunt that lived next to granny had an in-ground pool in the backyard, but I didn't want to swim in it if anyone else was in the water. I hung on tight to the sides of the pool and didn't veer far from the ladder.

My aunt's four girls decided to initiate me into their new pool. I was timidly doggy-paddling near one of ladders when they jumped in and circled me like vultures. As the youngest and smallest girl, I struggled to defend myself. They took turns dunking me until I just about drowned. Each cousin held me under water until I felt my nostrils burning with chlorine and my brain exploding. I sprang up to catch a breath, but then the next cousin and then the next continued dunking me, taking turns in a circle until I didn't come up any more. Finally, they pulled me up and tossed me off to the side of the pool where I hunched over spitting and puking up water. The oldest girl was tasked to make sure nobody drowned in the pool. Of course, all our parents were inside smoking, drinking, and playing poker. Mom didn't drink or smoke, but she was a fierce and competitive card player, so she was just as distracted as the rest of them.

I wasn't about to tattle-tell on my cousins for fear of what they could do to me next. During subsequent visits I stayed out of the pool unless they chased me and threw me in. But, as I grew and became stronger, I was able to hold my own against them in baseball, kickball, and dodge ball. I could hit a baseball or kick more home runs than anyone who played, including any parent who occasionally participated in the cousins' games. Later in life, I overcame my tremendous fear of the water by taking lessons and swimming a mile a day.

**

In my early twenties, a neighbor asked me to do a tarot card reading with her. She was a student finishing up her PhD thesis in Astrology and needed another guinea pig for a research project. I was afraid to know what she would see in my future. I certainly didn't want her to know about my childhood. I had no faith in card readers and thought they were a bunch of crack pots. I'd heard growing up that bible said attempting to predict the future was devil's work. I didn't want to mess with another devil in my life. However, my neighbor appeared reasonable and intelligent. After some discussion, I wanted to help her and decided to go along with the card reading.

She looked at the cards and told me that I was susceptible to drowning and needed to be careful around water. I thought about my grandfather drowning in the Ohio River and how horrible it must be to suffocate to death. I'd already gotten two a glimpse of what it would feel like to drown, and I would later get a third.

In my thirties I became interested in kayaking when I moved to Georgia. A co-worker told me beautiful stories about the rivers and mountains in Georgia. I had canoed with my brother Dan in the Alafia River in Florida a couple times and loved being in the nature. I decided to take a kayaking lesson from my co-worker's husband. After a lot of resistance and telling her about my near drowning experiences in the pools, she talked me into taking the lesson. She insisted that her husband had a lot of experience teaching beginners how to kayak and would take good care of me.

One drizzly cold Saturday morning, the husband Mike and I headed to Altoona Lake near Red Top Mountain in Georgia to begin the lesson. The kayak resembled a coffin with a hole on top within which to squeeze your body into. A brace under the hole locks your legs into the kayak so you can use your body weight to roll, if needed. Basically, your body sits in the kayak like a tight peg in a board. You can move your arms and twist your trunk, but that's it. A neoprene skirt wraps under the hole and cinches tightly around your waist so you don't fill the boat with water if you flip over.

Instructor Mike taught me to wet exit in the calm water of the lake. A wet exit is when you flip the kayak over, pull the tight neoprene skirt off the lip of the hole, get your legs out from under the brace by pushing on the sides of the boat with force, and wiggle your rear end out of the kayak. Pretty simple, right? I tried the wet exit technique several times and finally managed to get out of the kayak without help.

The next part of the session in the lake involved rolling the kayak completely over so you don't have to get your ass out of the boat. It certainly saves tons of time to just flip, roll, and keep moving. But I couldn't get the hang of rolling to save my life. While upside down with water pouring into your nose and soaking your brain, you are supposed to contort your body, position the paddle perfectly under the water, and fling yourself up with all the strength you can muster using the force of paddle through the water. I didn't master that lesson. I didn't roll a single time. I got worn out from flipping, flopping, and snorting water.

Now, it was time to put the one-hour lesson into action. The next step was to load the kayaks and launch them into the class II rapids in the Etowah River at Castleberry Bridge. An inner voice loudly told me not to do it. As we got closer to the river it kept repeating itself like the beat of my heart and wouldn't stop.

I kept telling the instructor that I'd had enough. I was tired and wanted to call it a day. Even the dark cloudy sky and cold rain didn't keep him from insisting I give it a try. He kept saying, "You get wet in the river rain or shine." He was determined to get the kayaks in the river, and he wasn't going to let me spoil his fun.

Because I had taken too much time trying to learn how to get out of the kayak while under water and not mastering the death roll, we were behind Mike's schedule. He decided not to put the kayaks in the original easy starting point at Castleberry Bridge. Instead, we pulled off the side of the road and unloaded the kayaks next to a class I rapid.

He geared me up with the neoprene skirt, helped me squeeze into the kayak, and pushed me from the shore into the rapid with my boat pointing the wrong way, up river. As he shoved me into the river, he told me to eddy, and then spin out and he would meet me down the river. I didn't know what the "F" he was talking about. He might as well have been speaking French. He sounded like Charlie Brown's parents…blah…blah…blah… as he barked out more orders while I'm unsteadily balancing on the pinnacle of a backward flowing wave.

'Spin out!' he yelled.

'What does that mean?' I yelled back.

'Lean over and go down river.'

I leaned to the wrong side. The wave immediately flipped me over. I dangled upside down with water rushing me down stream. I tried to use the paddle and contort my body forward to flip myself over. I got my face right to the bottom edge of the top of the river and could see the sky but couldn't get any higher to catch a breath. Underwater, I let go of the paddle and tried to pull the neoprene skirt off the lip. I couldn't find the handle. The skirt wouldn't release. My body got caught in underbrush. I was trapped.

I began floating through a tunnel. I could see vivid spectrums of blue and a light drawing me nearer. I was full of joy. I couldn't see myself but felt my spirit moving through space. I was alone but knew that I wouldn't be for long. I was going home. I was at peace, in the most peaceful place that I have ever been or ever experienced. Just like I have always told Mom, "We will all be together again someday." I have faith.

Except it wasn't my time to go. If I went, who'd watch out for Mom? I woke up puking my guts out on the shore as my instructor resuscitated me. I cried so hard that I shivered for days. I couldn't stop shaking. I'd met drowning head on and was no longer afraid.

Years ago, I heard a five-year-old say, "You have to "wissen" (listen) to your body and do what it tells you to do." Next time, I hope I have enough sense to listen when the thunder roars.

* * *

During another visit to my aunt's house, the girl cousins got a hold of my uncle's straight edge shaving razor, pinned me down, and shaved my fuzzy legs. They cut my skinny knobby knees with the razor. I thought the hair would grow back in a day or two and Mom wouldn't find out. Luck wasn't with me that day. Mom saw me runnin' with bloody knees and asked me to come to the poker table. She bent down and starred at my naked stick legs and said "Wha'd ja git into?" I started sweating and got tongue tied. I knew I would be in for a good whoopin'. I said, "I don't know." She examined them further and said, "Why didn't you ask me if you could shave your legs?" I said. "I don't know." She said, "Go tell your father what you did." Obviously, "I don't know" was not the right answer.

Dad handed out corporal punishment for most any infraction. It didn't take much to push him over the edge to exercise a whoopin'. He walked around with one hand on his belt just waiting for a fast draw opportunity.

I eased down to the pool area where Dad was standing with an uncle. I nervously swallowed and felt a rock in my stomach that would sink me if I jumped into the pool. Temporarily drowning may be a better punishment than what I was about to receive. "Just drown me and wake me up when it's over," I'd say to myself. Little did I know that I would get plenty of that later on down the road.

We weren't allowed to talk to our parents if they were having a conversation with an adult. Be seen and not heard. Speak only when spoken to.

I just stood close enough to Dad knowing that he knew why I was there…to plead my case. Been there before.

'Why aren't ya playin'?' Dad asked.

'Mom sent me because I shaved my legs.'

'Ya old enough?'

'No.' I said.

'Did someone put ya up to it?'

'No!' I lied, started crying while gasping for air.

I could hear the leather sail off the polyester pants. It sounded like a basketball going straight through the net without touching the rim, swoosh! Dad would double up the belt and hold it in one hand while grabbing both of my wrists with the other hand. Round and round in a circle we'd go, in front of God and everyone. I tried to run like hell after freeing one hand to cover my skinny little ass from the blasts. The harder I ran, the faster he would deliver the blows. I was his tetherball.

I couldn't determine how Dad decided enough licks had been distributed. I think it depended on how much alcohol he had in him. He must have stopped when he got dizzy and was ready to puke or pass out from spinning in a circle.

'This hurts me more than it hurts you.' He yelled with 180 pounds of force striking a fifty-five-pound bony little body with zero fat screaming and whaling bloody murder. I wasn't about to stand there and take it without protesting, so I screamed, just like Mom would have.

For my dad's generation, there wasn't an option to go to your room for time out. There was no patience for an explanation from the accused, or for attempts to negotiate a plea bargain. If you tried to defend yourself, you got it that much more. When a situation progressed to the level of "go tell your father," that was it. Standing in front of Dad, you told a quick abridged version of your accused crime, were immediately sentenced, and punishment was delivered swiftly. Then, you were expected to get over it just as quickly and get on with your playing without crying about it anymore.

It must have been a conspiracy because all my cousins got whoopin's too. Even though we didn't talk about it, we witnessed it. My new generation secretly vowed that stripes on the legs wouldn't be delivered to our kids. Just hide and watch we'd say (meaning wait and see). We will make whoopin's come to an end someday when we have our own kids. We won't beat our kids; we will be friends with them and play together. No more "kids are to be seen and not heard." The new generation of kids will have a voice, we'll make sure of it, just watch, you'll see.

*　*　*

While the poker game continued, the women took turns cooking hamburgers and hotdogs on the grill. They pulled corn out of the field, shucked it, and then boiled it in a big steel pot on the stove. The women sliced fresh tomatoes, onions, cucumbers, and lettuce from the

Left-Right-Left

garden, and they rolled out dough for a homemade apple pie to accompany the hand-cranked ice cream for dessert.

One of the women always laid a newspaper on the picnic table and sliced a big watermelon in two-inch round sections, then into quarter sections for easy handling for us to eat after dinner.

Dad was the first to start a watermelon seed fight. He'd place a watermelon seed between his thumb and forefinger and squeeze it so hard that it propelled through the air to hit your body. The landing was impossible to predict because the slippery seeds excelled in every direction. Once the first seed launched, a full force seed fight between the kids and Dad began, then the kids against each other. Throughout life Mom said, "I had to raise four kids and one of them was your father."

After dinner, homemade ice cream and pie, watermelon and chasing lightening bugs after dark, the adult poker game really heated up. We'd pass the poker table while tearing through the house since we had to stay inside after the sun set. The beer flowed all day at my aunt's house but when the night approached; the moonshine jug got passed around with lots of swiggin' going on.

You could tell when my uncle Lemual had too much to drink because his eye glasses slanted on his face. He'd pull a pistol out of his pocket, just like a pocket knife, and start showing it off. I was his favorite niece and he made me feel special. He called me "Blondie." I admired my uncle, who was a veteran of the Korean War like my dad. He didn't talk about the war, but I knew he had gotten all shot up, taking many bullets in his stomach. He put his own life at risk for the freedom many take for granted.

He made an offer to my parents to adopt me so I could go to college for free because he was a 100% rated disabled veteran. The enormous sacrifice he'd made allowed his children and spouse to go to college for free. All of his kids graduated from college. I was in my teens at the time, and I didn't know about the adoption offer until many years later. Mom and Dad didn't think it was a good idea. I always appreciated that he and my aunt Joy saw potential in me and were willing to help.

Visiting from northern Ohio, another uncle, this one a WWII and Korean War Veteran, and aunt were also gathered around the poker table. I stopped for a minute to watch the game. That uncle was swiggin' moonshine like there was no tomorrow. I saw him get up from the chair and hit my aunt over the head with a beer bottle. She fell to the floor with blood squirting out the top of her head onto the yellow linoleum floor. Adults scrambled to help her and pull my uncle off her as he was beating her bleeding head in. At this point I knew that we weren't the only ones in the world with a wife beating drunkard monstrous Dad.

6

Fish

When we got back to the city from granny's house, we had to change our accent back to one of a Yankee. We quickly picked up our cousins' accent in Kentucky. Instead of saying "Over there," they would say "Oh var." If we spoke with an Appalachian twang in

Lincoln Park the kids would make fun of us. If we spoke like a Yankee in Kentucky, they would tease us too. We learned to talk the talk in either setting.

Things were going well for a change. We had enough money to live on. Dad got tired of fishing on the pier, and against Mom's wishes, he came home one day pulling an aluminum Jon boat with two bench seats.

A Jon boat is good for fishing in calm water. It's unstable in a storm and rides over the top of waves rather than cutting through them because it doesn't have a V bottom. Dad's Jon boat sported a big outboard motor mounted on the back. When Dad took us fishing, my brothers and I were instructed to sit on the front bench to add weight to the front of the boat. The motor was so heavy that that front of the Jon boat stuck out of the water.

One summer day in 1970, Dad took my brothers and me out for a day of fishing for walleye and trout on Lake Huron, which converges with the Detroit River and Lake Erie. We drove to Lake Huron because Dad said, "Detroit River's full of oil and shit."

Lake Erie was, too. In 1969 the Cuyahoga River that runs into Lake Erie had caught fire from dumping sewage and industrial chemicals into the Great Lakes. Soon after the "Mistake on the Lake" happened in Cleveland, the oil-matted Rouge River in Detroit caught fire too, shooting flames fifty feet in the air. The Rouge River flows into the Detroit River. In 1968, the Detroit River was the chief contributor of organic substances, phenols, oils, coliform organisms, and other sewage wastes that freely ran into Lake Erie. Not even the population's imminent death from typhoid fever, cholera, or lead poisoning from water pipes induced Americans to spend money to treat their water supply or their sewage. Because of this and many other sources of continuing pollution, the waters of Lake Erie were toxic.

Mom packed us plenty of bologna sandwiches, snacks, and water for the day. She didn't like boats or fishing so she stayed home. We proudly toted bright new orange life jackets and fishing poles as Dad loaded all the gear into the Ford Country Squire station wagon.

We stopped at a store to purchase worms and gas for the boat motor and filled up an extra red metal can of gas to spare. Dad also bought two six packs of beer and put them in the white Styrofoam cooler. He made sure Mom didn't see him leaving the house with any alcohol.

Dad backed the Jon boat down a ramp at a park along the Detroit River and navigated us toward Lake Huron. It was a beautiful sunny day on the water and everyone but me caught lots of fish. I wouldn't put a worm on my hook because I thought it would hurt the worm and I couldn't stand the guts that spewed out from hooking it. I baited my hook by rolling up little balls of bread from my boloney sandwich.

Hours passed by and we were having a lot of fun navigating in and out of coves and seeing all kinds of birds. By this time, the food and water were all gone. Dad put the fish in the cooler after he ran out of beer.

As we approached another boat, Dad waved at the men to come over to us. He convinced the men in the other boat to trade a six pack of their beer for all our fish, taking no objections from his crew of kids. He handed them our cooler full of fresh catch and they forked over the six pack. My brothers and I started worrying. We knew what alcohol did to Dad and were afraid to say anymore because we could end up in the bottom of the river if we mouthed off.

Now, it was getting late. We could barely see the sun over the horizon. A storm was brewing up quickly and the waves were getting bigger and bigger and rocking the boat side to side. It started pouring rain. Dad passed out in the bottom of the boat. We shook and shook him and told him to get up. He just lay there snoring, oblivious to the storm.

Dennis Jr. started the motor and said we had to get to shore. There was no shore in sight. In complete darkness, Dennis Jr. attempted to position the boat so we wouldn't get tossed over into the cold black water. We slowly began to rock over top of one wave after another as they crashed over the front of the boat spilling water onto the deck. The waves started coming faster and more powerful. Danny and I held on for dear life by wrapping our arms around the wooded bench seat, shivering from the cold and softly crying in fear. We didn't want to break Dennis Jr.'s concentration while he tried to keep the boat in line with the breaking waves.

We watched Dennis Jr.'s every move as he turned the motor's handle so the boat's flat front smacked the top of the waves while he tried so hard to save us. We were going nowhere in a hurry, but Dennis Jr. kept the boat from turning over. We feared for our lives. I just knew that we would be dead soon. I prayed and prayed to Jesus to save us.

I looked up and by some miracle a spot light was moving back and forth across the water. The U.S. Coast Guard shined the light on our little Jon boat as we screamed for help. The U.S. Coast Guard lifted my brothers and me out of the little Jon boat, put us in their boat and brought us to shore where Mom was standing in the rain at the boat ramp crying hard as we ran into her arms. I don't remember what happened to Dad. He didn't go to jail, so he must have talked his way out of almost drowning all of us.

* * *

After the fishing outing, Dad seemed to go into a deep depression. He stayed in the basement talking on the Ham radio and having less interaction with the rest of us.

I was old enough to have responsibilities now. I made my bed (as I had done for years already) but now I had to make my brother's beds too. I protested. For the life of me, I couldn't understand why they couldn't make their own beds. It made me mad that I had to clean up after them when they were more than capable.

I folded the clothes in the dryer, dusted, cleared the table, dried the dishes, and performed other household duties that my brothers didn't have to do because it was considered girls' work. It felt like they didn't have to do anything except get up from the table where they left their dirty dishes. I started getting an attitude.

If Mom made hamburgers and French fries and the ketchup wasn't within either of my brothers' reach (and was near me), they hollered, "Gimme the ketchup." I asked them to say "please" but they refused. I just sat there and ignored them as they repeated the "gimmie,

gimmie, gimmie, Mom make her gimmie" until one of my parents told me to pass the ketchup. I didn't take orders from my brothers and held my ground.

During the remainder of the summer of fourth grade, next-door neighbor Donna Holcomb "baby" sat us while Mom worked and Dad trucked the highway. Donna made lunch and didn't curtail our adventures. We were just fine with her as a baby sitter. For the most part, she sat on the front stoop while we played outside.

One day, Donna brought her new boyfriend over while baby sitting and he sat on the stoop with her. The space was tight. She got up, bent over and stuck her rear end through the storm door and glass shattered everywhere. Donna wasn't hurt, but that was the end of the babysitting period. Mom felt like we didn't need a baby sitter anymore if the baby sitter was getting into more trouble than we were getting into. Things were about to change, again.

Winter was upon us. Dad was working less and less and holing up in the basement. We started hearing about money problems. Dennis Jr. got a paper route to make some money. Dennis Jr., Danny and I went door to door on weekends asking people if we could shovel the snow in their driveways. We didn't get turned away, so we shoveled until we couldn't shovel anymore for a quarter each for one driveway. We work hard because we wanted to have money to buy candy and little toys that our parents couldn't afford anymore.

When we weren't shoveling driveways, we were building snowmen and igloos in the backyard. We started a club in the top of the garage rafters in a tiny area where we could barely stand up. The price to join the club was a quarter. I was the treasurer. The money was used to buy snacks at Open Pantry. Mom always had plenty of snacks for us to eat, but we wanted to buy jiffy pop popcorn. Mom owned an electric popcorn maker that we forbidden to use because hot oil in the bottom of the appliance that popped the corn and could burn us.

After we walked to Open Pantry with our neighborhood friends Tim and Brenda, we bought the popcorn that comes in a tin pan with a long handle for holding over a stove-top. Then we headed back to the garage to build a fire in the rafters. First, Dennis Jr. searched and found matches in Dad's shop in the basement. We were ready to start popping and could already taste the delicious hot buttery and salty popcorn before the fire was even built by just thinking about it.

Dennis Jr. stacked sticks up in a pile but couldn't get the wet limbs to catch fire with the small pack of matches. He got some newspaper from the house thinking it would dry out the sticks. The paper caught on fire right away and worked like a dream, until it started catching other things on fire, like the cardboard box full of Christmas lights. Dennis Jr. tried to stomp out the fire, but it had spread too quickly.

We flew out of the rafters, jumped onto the garage floor and ran screaming to the house that the garage caught itself on fire. Dad was home and had enough time to put the fire out with the water hose with minimal damage. We got lucky. That was the end of the rafter club. We didn't get a-whoopin' over it. I guess not getting torched was enough drama for that day.

7

Beatings

Dad kept on trucking down the road for a while and rarely home. His absence seemed to help regulate the emotional upheaval in the house. Mom worked at "Monkey Wards" (Montgomery Ward, Inc.) and attempted to collect money from "dead beats." Mom titled herself a "dun" collector. Dun is an early 1600's word. A person who duns another makes a demand for payment from them. At Montgomery Ward, Mom dunned "dead beats" by telephone.

Montgomery Ward started off as a mail-order business in 1872 and stayed in business until they liquidated in 2001. The business model basically resembles online shopping today. The founder Aron Montgomery Ward initially targeted rural customers who wanted "city" goods. At the time, rural people's main access to merchandise was through general stores in their home towns. Ward's business philosophy was built on cutting out the middleman to reduce costs and provide a large variety of goods to rural Americans.

Customers received a catalog in the mail, affectionately called a "wish book," that contained over 10,000 items spread across 240 pages. We dreamed about ordering goods in the catalog and would turn down the corners of the pages for stuff we wanted. The catalog was part of our household and sat on top of the coffee table.

To get the goods, people in rural areas selected items from the catalog, filled out a form, wrote a check for payment, and sent the form and check through the mail to Montgomery Ward to place the order. Days or weeks later, the merchandise arrived at their doorstep. In the beginning, customers picked up the goods from the nearest train station.

Mom worked in an office at a retail store in Lincoln Park. She inched her way up to supervising two other women whose job was to collect payments that were only a little late. Mom dunned the hard to crack nuts. Her southern accent, intelligence, and wit convinced people to send in a payment for merchandise that was used up or long gone.

Mom went to work every day in beautiful pants suits, a dress, or a skirt, blouse and jacket with a beehive hairdo that was "done up" at a local beauty parlor every week. Mom was a proud business woman, impeccable at her job, and took her job responsibilities seriously. At the kitchen dinner table, she would tell us stories about how she would get someone to pay their overdue bill. Basically, if she couldn't get them to pay the whole bill, she would convince them to send a check with a minimum payment. If they made a minimum payment, the customer would be in good standing with the store and could charge some more! When they found that out, they were happy to pay. Acquiring stuff and not having to pay for it right away created plenty of jobs for Dunn collectors.

We were living the American Dream, or so it seemed to others. We actually lived caught in the middle of two distinct cultures, north and south. Mom tried hard to take us up in social status while she worked and earned income that she spent on us. We lived in a middle-class suburb, attended a great school, wore fashionable clothes, and had new bicycles, roller skates, skateboards, ice skates, and lots of toys and board games to play from Mom's additional income.

As Mom prospered in her job, Dad tried even harder to take us down when he was drinking. He would make degrading comments to Mom like, "You're gittin' too big for your britches." Dad would have been happy with us living in an old ratty trailer in the middle of nowhere. "You can take Billy out of the hills, but you can't take the hills out of Billy." This saying I heard growing up proved to be true in our house.

On the home front and in school, things seemed to be clicking right along for the most part. Dennis Jr. and Danny played pee wee baseball and I played outfield on a t-ball team. Like good patriotic American families, my brothers joined cub scouts, and I became a Bluebird, which was the younger version of a Camp Fire Girl.

The Camp Fire Girl (CFG) program was designed to encourage strength, compassion, and wisdom in young girls and was a strong basis for allowing us to recognize the importance of self-respect, service to our community and country, and openness to diversity in others and the environment as a whole.

CFG fostered programs that encouraged young girls, beginning in World War II. The vintage Camp Fire book describes a CFG as someone with high ideals, a quiet pride in being a girl, deep love for her country, a good friend, has interests and hobbies enjoyed with others and alone, has good health, good habits, and a love for the outdoors. Mom found this organization and took me to the meetings. I met new friends and Mom found other women that she enjoyed talking with as they shared stories about their families. The CFG's program gave Mom and me a platform that we could share adventures with just the two of us. We enjoyed this wonderful experience together until things started going south again at home.

***

Dad and Mom made new friends and together they played a card game called Canasta. Canasta rules resemble Rummy 500 but scoring is different. The couple's kids were too young for my brothers and me to play with so we watched TV while our parents played cards until we fell asleep on the couch. They played for hours and Dad drank for hours.

The clock turned later and later, way past our bedtime. Dad woke me up from sleeping on the couch and carried me out to the car. He said I was playing possum and should walk. I could smell the alcohol on his breath. Charismatic, charming, "good time Dennis" didn't show his violent behavior in public, except for this one night.

My brothers were piled in the back seat of the station wagon lying down to sleep. I sat in the middle of the front bench seat. Mom insisted on driving because Dad staggered to the car. He insisted on driving. He had to be in control. He grabbed the car key from Mom and fumbled at getting behind the wheel.

I was wide awake and white knuckled watching the car swerve into the opposite lane, back into our lane, off the road and back into our lane again repeatedly as he went faster and faster. Mom started grabbing the wheel trying to get the car back into our lane. She kept telling Dad to pull over because he was going to kill us all. He wouldn't stop, kept telling her to shut up, and yelled that he saw her "playing footsie" under the card table with the other man. He drove even faster and more reckless. He was trying to kill us all. Then Mom started grabbing the ignition switch attempting to turn the car off as it veered from one side of the road to the other. I watched in shock and fear as both parents' hands gripped the wheel and the car swerved around oncoming traffic.

Finally, Mom turned the ignition switch off and the car came to an abrupt stop along the road in a neighborhood. Dad got out of the car, stumbled over to the passenger side and dragged Mom out of the car by the hair of her head and beat her with his fists in the front yard of someone's house until she was knocked to the ground screaming. She laid in the yard curled in a ball on her knees trying to cover her head while he punched her entire body and repeatedly kicked her deformed and disable leg that had been previously destroyed in an accident, twice.

Then, he jumped on her back and began crushing her skull with his fists. My brothers and I tried like hell to pull him off her. He got ahold of us and we flew through the air with each attempt.

Finally, before he could kill her, a porch light came on. A man walked onto the porch and didn't say a word. The beating stopped and the man walked back inside, not willing to come out and help three small shell-shocked children and a severely beaten woman laid out in his front yard and unable to stand up. But the porch light stopped the beating. There was no cell phone to call the police. Mom crawled back to the car and pulled herself in as my brothers and I guided her. We entered the back seat and crouched down on the floorboard behind the front seats praying to God who led us home.

For years I wanted Dad locked up in jail and the key thrown away. Why couldn't someone save us from this monster? After every beating, the next day Dad exhibited selective amnesia. It was a pattern. He acted overly playful and happy after each explosion.

Behind the bedroom door, I would hear him promise Mom that "it" would never happen again. He didn't acknowledge this unconscionable behavior or apologize to my brothers and me. Instead he would take us on a day trip to Cedar Point (amusement park) and allowed us to bring a friend, or be a little more lenient when we wanted a toy from the store. He'd affectionately use his nicknames for us when he was in a good mood. Dennis Jr.'s was "June Bug." My nickname was "Sissy" or "Teri Bug." Danny's was "Little Man," and later "Dan the Man."

When Dad was away for a couple weeks in the semi-truck, a great big card showed up in the mail telling us how much he missed us and that he would be home soon. Occasionally, he brought home toys from a truck stop. I still have the small metal collectible Chitty Chitty Bang Bang car, with wings that spread out with the touch of a lever and smiling passengers waving their arms in the air. I call it the "Shitty Shitty Bang-Bang Car." One of the kids got tossed out of the car during a move and was never found again. It sits on my dresser with a hole in the back seat where the missing child used to sit.

Dad put a basketball hoop on the garage. That was the best day of my life. I played H.O.R.S.E. with my brothers and other neighborhood kids from sunrise to sunset. I played this game a thousand times using different words. As a teenager, they were usually cuss words.

When Dad was home from trucking and needed to sleep during the day before heading out on another week-long journey, if I was outside shooting, he'd holler out the window for me to stop bouncing the ball. I was obsessed with playing basketball and wouldn't stop no matter what the consequences might be.

I practiced throwing the ball through the center of the rim without touching it and running like crazy to catch the ball before it bounced and made noise so when Dad was home, I could keep playing. I had to run fast because we didn't have a net on the rim.

Playing basketball became my saving grace. I played competitively in high school and on a traveling team while in the U.S. Air Force. I could consistently sink 49 out of 50 free throws from so many years of practicing.

My brothers and I had plenty of friends. We played games like hide-and-seek, four-square, tag, and dodge ball. We walked on top of the chain-link fences that divided the back yards of each suburban neighborhood without falling off. We ran to the fence, grabbed the bottom, and flipped our feet over the top, like doing a cartwheel over the fence to get away from someone chasing us when playing tag. We climbed to the top of large oak trees, jumped onto the garage roof, and jumped off without fear or injury.

From abandoned wood in a field, we built a raft like Tom Sawyer had and floated down the South Branch Ecorse River that leads into the Detroit River without ever getting caught or drowning from it falling apart, all without life jackets.

We rode bikes for miles collecting bottles and turned them in for cash at the Open Pantry convenience store a few blocks away. We used the money to buy candy.

Mostly, Danny was too young to play with us or often to sick. He was no bigger than a minnow in a fishin' pond. I called him "minner." One day he was riding his Big Wheeler to Open Pantry to turn in bottles and collect money. We always rode our bikes to Open Pantry. We didn't know going there was against the rules. Only this time Dad stopped him. He stopped the car, opened the trunk, pulled out an electric extension cord and whipped little sickly asthmatic Danny with the long black cord. He came home with bruises, welts, and blood all over his body. Not even the weak and sick were given mercy from the wickedness of the devil.

Dad had good qualities too when he was not depressed. In the summer, the ice cream truck could be heard from a long way up the road. This gave us plenty of time to ask Dad if he would buy us an ice cream. We ran into the basement when we heard the ice cream truck song. He usually gave each of us a quarter for an ice cream. We ran outside squealing with delight hoping and praying that the ice cream truck hadn't already passed our house. Dennis Jr. and Danny usually got a drum stick and I tried something different each time like a strawberry shortcake, king cone, dreamsicle, or a rainbow pop-up. We never knew if Dad was going to be up or down when asking for

Left-Right-Left

something. If he was down, he just said, "No." We knew better than to ask again and quickly ran back outside to play.

*　*　*

Dennis Jr. and I crossed a divided highway and walked our bikes through the intersection to get to the "nothing but candy store." A quarter filled up a paper sac with wax bottles, wax lips, pixie sticks, jaw breakers, candy cigarettes, taffy, candy buttons, sweet tarts, twizzlers, and hundreds of other selections. We never got caught going that far from home.

All the neighborhood kids loved to play at our house. Dad got a couple of men to finish the basement by putting dark brown paneling on the walls and adding a drop ceiling. In our new "family" room, we played games and watched TV. Dad's sweat equity and Mom's extra income paid for the renovation. It got us out of Mom's hair too.

When one of Dad's favorite bars went out of business, he bought the coin operated 1965 Bally Bowler bowling alley with swivel action pins in addition to two pinball machines; one was a Lucky Strike. The pins on the Bally Bowler would fly in all directions when the 4.5-inch diameter hard rubber balls hit the metal reactors on the surface below. The pins snapped to the top and the other pins would remain for the next throw, just like real bowling. The bowling machine took up a good section of the new family room.

We were the only kids in town to have a bowling and pin ball machines in our basement. The neighborhood kids wanted to come to our house to play when it rained. Snow didn't keep us inside, but the rain did.

Dad enjoyed playing games and taught us how to play card games like Solitaire, Kings Corners, Hearts, Poker, and Rummy 500. We also played board games when it rained like Battleship, Monopoly, Checkers, Dominos, Clue, Operation, The Game of Life, Dominos, Yahtzee, Sorry, and Cribbage.

But usually, we stayed outside until Mom rang the dinner bell. Sometimes at dusk before dinner, we chased the mosquito spraying truck on our bikes through the neighborhood. It's a wonder we don't glow in the dark when the lights are off.

Dad had a shop on the other side of the family room adjacent to the laundry room. He spent hours fixing electronic devices, like other people's TV's, by testing and replacing tubes. He bought all kinds of gadgets for his workshop. He also liked to watch TV with us in the basement, but only shows like Gunsmoke, Bonanza, The Beverly Hill Billy's, Petticoat Junction, Green Acres, McHale's Navy, Gomer Pyle U.S.M.C., or The Andy Griffin Show.

He couldn't stand watching That Girl, Bewitched, I dream of Jeanie, or I Love Lucy. If I Love Lucy was playing and he could hear it, he would come into the family room and change the channel, telling us not to watch that trash. In the 1970's, the Mary Tyler Moore show struck him the same way. He didn't like bossy or sassy women.

When Hee Haw was first aired in 1969, you'd have thought that he died and gone to heaven." If Dad was home that show played on our TV every time it aired. Hee Haw was centered on country music and the rural culture similar to Dad's people back home in the Appalachian Mountains. Dad felt at home watching the show. Hee Haw was equally well known for its voluptuous, scantily clad women in stereotypical farmer's daughter outfits and country-style minidresses (a group that came to be known as the "Hee Haw Honeys"). I couldn't stand watching the show and went to my room to read when it aired. Even as a kid, I thought the show was degrading and made women look stupid.

When Dad had free time, he talked on an amateur radio, also called a Citizen Band (CB) radio. His handle was "Crazyhorse." He proudly showed everyone his amateur radio license. According to Dad, the license gave him permission to talk to people all over the world on a Ham radio.

His Ham radio antenna reached the clouds. The bottom was attached to the side of our house. You could see it from miles away on the suburb blocks of Lincoln Park. We'd be watching our favorite Saturday morning TV cartoons like The Flintstones, Scooby Doo, Bugs Bunny, or the Jetson's when Dad's voice wiped the picture and sound from the TV. This could happen anytime of day or night. When he keyed the microphone to talk on the radio, the signal was so strong that horizontal lines went through the entire TV screen and bounced as he talked. As his voice sounded through the TV, wiggly static lines flew across the picture tube like stock market charts gone mad. His voice penetrated the entire neighborhood's block of TV enjoyment. Over and over he would repeat, "Breaker breaker one niner, this is Crazyhorse, got a copy on that?"

When the phone started ringing off the hook, Mom answered and took the neighbors' wrath of telling her to get Dad off the radio so they could watch TV without static lines running across the screen. Dad would say, "What makes 'em think it's me? It's not my fault that somethings wrong with their TV." He couldn't hide the 65-feet-high antenna attached to our house, but he wasn't about to take ownership that he could possibly interfere with other people's electronic equipment. Dad didn't like to admit his faults.

The Carol Burnett show was popular then. Dad hated Carol Burnett. He couldn't tolerate "bossy" women. When he found out someone complained about interrupting the Carol Burnett show, he made sure that his mouth didn't stop running for the entire episode. He did the same thing during the I Love Lucie show, too. We weren't allowed to watch those "bossy" women on TV.

Mom stopped answering the phone. She didn't care how long Dad yacked on the radio because it made him happy. She didn't have time to watch TV herself and didn't want to be bothered by all the commotion it caused. She had enough going on already. If Dad was happy, then he was good Dad and not bad Dad. Talking on the radio kept Dad out of the bars. Eventually Mom got our phone number changed and had it unlisted from the phone book.

Dad said that Crazyhorse was a famous Indian and that my great-great grandmother was a Cherokee/Blackfoot Indian. He was proud of the fact that he was one quarter Cherokee Indian.

He often said, "I have some Blackfoot In-gin' in me from my great granny." He said, "Her name's 'Frizzy' and buried in Logan, Ohio. She couldn't be buried in the Darnell cemetery with the rest of the kin cuz she was In-gin'. That wasn't allowed back then." I found a picture of "Frizzy" in our family album. The back of the picture said "Mary Frazie." She didn't look like an Indian to me.

Dad said, "I can't grow hair on my chest because I'm part "In-gin'." In-gin's don't have hair on their chest." He said it with confidence, like the hair should have sprouted up like a Chia pet if he wasn't an "In-gin'."

***

Dad's basement workshop had enough watts of electricity to kill a cow. He warned us to not go behind the Ham radio and mess around because we could get hurt.

One day it was raining outside so we were stuck inside playing. Mom had just finished painting the entire unfinished part of the basement floor battleship gray. She wasn't home from Monkey Wards yet. We strapped our adjustable metal hustler speed roller skates to our shoes and started creating a figure eight around Dad's workshop and the laundry area. A metal support beam held up the first floor of the house. We grabbed ahold of it and went around in circles squealing with joy, skating faster and faster. Because the light was so dim in the basement, we didn't notice the track marks in the paint we left behind with each lap.

I wanted to create a longer lap to skate and checked for space behind Dad's Ham radio station. I tripped on thick cables lying on the floor. I fell grabbing the top of the 220v cable that was connected to the Ham radio. The shock sent me flying through the air. Dad found out and thought it was funny when he got home. The shock caused me enough pain so none of us got a whoopin' for ruining the new paint job on the basement floor, although Mom wasn't happy because she was the one who did all the work.

8

Lessons

From the time Dennis Jr.'s feet hit the floor in the morning until getting into bed at night, he was on the go and getting into something. If he could find a way to get out the door, even if Mom locked the dead bolt, he was down the road before she could catch him. As a master escape artist, he couldn't be confined to the inside of a house. He climbed over fences before age two. When tall enough to get up a tree, he climbed to the top and onto the garage roof so he could jump into the neighbor's yard. Dennis Jr. couldn't sit still for a New York minute.

I was about eight years old. Mom dropped us off at the matinee to see 101 Dalmatians. We were living the American Dream with pop, candy bars, and popcorn to keep us busy while watching the animated movie. Dennis Jr. kept getting up and throwing popcorn. He eventually got kicked out of the theater. When Mom pulled up at the curb in front of the theater an attendant told her not to bring him back again without her being there too.

This was the only hour and a half that she had to herself to go to the grocery store and get her bee hive hair done up. Mom had the patience of a saint with us and didn't tell Dad about all our misbehaving. But with Dennis Jr. getting kicked out of the theater, her bucket tipped that day. She said, "I'll have to tell your father what you did." We all knew what that meant and it wasn't pretty.

Mom had a system. When she had enough of us, she'd say, "Don't make me tell your father." That meant we'd better settle down. If we didn't settle down, she'd say, "I'm going to tell your father when he gets home." That meant we had been warned several times to stop fighting, running in and out of the house, or anything else that got on her fragile nerves. But often we just ignored the warnings.

Mom never, not once, laid a hand on us. She left the unnerving dirty work to Dad. Since he was gone trucking for days and weeks on end, her only form of punishment was to threaten us with his wrath. That certainly worked for me most of the time, but it rarely worked for Dennis Jr. He developed a stoic resistance and would receive his whoopin's without saying a word, crying out or shedding tears. I just tried to not get caught for getting into mischief.

Dennis Jr. was always in trouble. At times, Dad could be creative with his punishments. He had tried to teach Dennis Jr. Morse code, but Dennis Jr. wasn't interested in learning. Dad decided to administer it as a form of punishment for both brothers.

Dad owned a straight key to transmit Morse code. The Navy used Morse code as a method of transmitting textual information in a series of on-off tones. Each character had a unique sequence of dots and dashes. The straight key device consisted of a simple metal bar with a knob on top and a metal contact underneath it. The bar mounted on a piece of wood. When the bar contacted the metal, an electric circuit sounded a loud beep heard all over the house. He called it a "J38" which must have been some secret Navy acronym for "irritates the shit out of you." No wonder Dennis Jr. didn't like it.

Dad gave Dennis Jr. a piece of paper that had dots and dashes next to each letter in the alphabet. He gave him a quick lesson on how to operate the device and made him practice by reading the alphabet code, tapping the knob and striking the metal plate with quick or long contacts that created short or long shrilling dits and dahs. The metal plate was wired to a nine-volt battery that ignited the electric buzzer to sound a shrilling beep with each strike.

Remember touching that electric fence as a kid? You did it once and never did it again. Well, I pressed the knob on the J38 once and the shrill sent me through the roof. Dad insisted on hearing every beep anywhere inside the house. Dennis Jr. would dit-dit-dah-dit for hours on end in the tiny finished attic bedroom while Dad hollered from the basement telling him what sentence to dit dah next. I didn't know what he was coding.

Dad stayed in the unfinished part of the dark basement talking on his Ham radio to anyone in the world who would listen to him, at all hours of the day and night. From the basement, he would yell to Dennis Jr. that he wasn't transcribing correctly. When he heard silence, he would yell for him to keep practicing. I don't know what was worse, the dit-dah-dits or the constant yelling from Dad. I do give Dad credit for trying something besides the belt.

* * *

Around fourth grade Dad was entertaining a local bar friend and smoking cigars in the basement. The guy's wife had recently given birth to a son so he was passing out free cigars. He called Dad his 'hillbilly friend' and Dad would call him a 'Michigander Pot Licker.' I thought a pot licker was someone who didn't get enough to eat. Later, I realized the pot was a toilet. Dad called himself a 'hillibilly' but nobody else could call him that unless they were one too.

We were watching Batman on TV and Dad hollered for us to get over there. He seemed to be in a jolly mood and was showing off all his electronic gadgets to his friend. He told each of us kids to take a big drag on the cigar and inhale it. He and his friend watched as each of us took a puff while he held it to our lips. When I inhaled the poisonous smoke, I started gagging, coughing, and vomiting. He laughed and said, "that'l cure ya' from ever wantin' to smoke." I didn't ever smoke, so maybe it did.

Dad's logic didn't apply to alcohol because every time we got a sore throat, Dad rubbed "Vicks sav" (Vicks VapoRub) on our throats, wrapped our necks with a hand towel, secured the towel with a large safety pin, and had us drink a shot of whiskey to cure us. We didn't ever go to the doctor, except for that Tetanus shot.

* * *

I collected pennies and kept them in a tall narrow cardboard cylinder. One time I picked up the cylinder to move it and it slipped through my hands and landed on my toe. It runs in the family for the toe next to the big toe to be longer than the rest. The cylinder caught that toe just right. My toe immediately began swelling and throbbing with pain. After not being able to walk for a couple days and complaining of the pain, Dad noticed that there was a big blood blister under the nail that was putting pressure on the nerves.

He took me to his shop in the basement, pulled out a tiny drill, screwed the smallest drill bit into it that he could find, and told me not to move as he squeezed my toe. He tried to drill a hole through the nail. For the first attempt, he used a toy drill that Dennis Jr. got for Christmas but the cheap plastic drill shook and didn't turn fast enough to go through my nail. Then, he pulled out the big gun to get the job done. Blood squirted out and I was immediately pain free. The nail eventually came off and grew another one twice as thick for the next time I dropped something on it.

***

For Christmas that year Santa brought Dennis Jr. and Danny hockey skates and me figure skates. We loved to ice skate. We slung the skates' laces around our necks and hiked to the Ecorse River, the same place where we built our Tom Sawyer raft.

Lions Park was located at end of our road and had a path to the river. The river didn't freeze hard at the edges. We had to delicately slide our butts onto the thin ice and work our way to the middle of the river where the ice was thicker.

We could hear the ice cracking under our bodies and see water seeping through the cracks as we lightly moved until we could stand up without falling through. I worried about drowning in the river. I had flashbacks from the summer pool flogging with my cousins and the big fat kid that sank me to the bottom of the public pool. It didn't keep me off the river though.

We skated so freely, forward and backwards. We jumped and spun in circles and played hockey on the ice. Our parents had no idea we were skating on the Ecorse River. But as much fun as we had with them, the ice skates had come with a heavy price to pay.

Mom and Dad had a cellar in the basement that was used to store canned goods in Mason jars. Dad told us and warned us several times not to go in the cellar. He reinforced the wooden latch on the door by pounding a nail in the latch then bending it into the door trim.

Dennis Jr. figured out that they were hiding our Christmas presents in the cellar. The suspense got the best of him. One early morning a couple weeks before Christmas he convinced Danny and me to take a peek in the cellar. Mom had already left for work. Dad was on the road trucking. We only had a few minutes to get out the door so we wouldn't be late for school. It was my job to make sure that we left for school on time.

I knew it wasn't right to go looking in the cellar. It was the worst decision that I ever made in my life. We darted like a pack of coyotes down the stairs sniffing over to the cellar door. Dennis Jr. bent the nail back and opened the wooden door. And to our surprise the cellar was full of unwrapped Christmas presents and toys that we were shocked to see. We didn't go in, but quickly shut the door. Dennis Jr. placed the nail back where he thought it was in the first place.

We always walked home from school, but that day and only that day, Dad was waiting for us in the station wagon in front of Carr elementary school. He saw us said, "Git over here!" I knew something was terribly wrong because I could see a crazy look in Dad's eyes. When I got inside the car I was scared to death. I felt like vomiting from the ice-cold silence until he said, "Ya know why I came to git ya?" I said, "No sir." He said, "Yur' bout' to find out." That's all he said.

When we got into the house, he told us to take all our clothes off and go to the basement because we were going to get a-whoopin'. I asked if we had to take off our underwear and he said we could leave it on. He told us that he warned us (and he did) not to go into the cellar, we didn't mind him, and we're going to get it good.

Dad lined us up in front of the cellar door, whipped off his belt like a gun coming out of John Wayne's holster and beat each of us one at time like a piñata. He held onto my skinny wrists with one hand as I ran around in circles trying to get away. He screamed at me to stand still and whaled on me until I could no longer stand. He had already finished with Dennis Jr. who tried to take it like a man by standing there while he was being pummeled. Danny was next and got a few licks.

Danny was puny for his age and always sick with asthma. Dad took mercy on him and told Dennis Jr. and me that "we mus' ta' put em' up to it cuz he was too young to know any better." With Dennis Jr. and me he drew blood. We displayed gashes, welts and bruises over our entire bodies for weeks, except he didn't strike our heads. He literally went crazy whipping us with his belt.

By the time he got to Danny he seemed to come back to his senses. We didn't talk about getting beat to each other. We were instructed to go to our rooms and stay there. I was afraid to come out to go to the bathroom, so I held it until Mom came home from work then quickly hid back in the closet of my room. I knew I would be dead if there was a round two. We didn't have dinner that night. I wouldn't have been able to eat anyway. I feared for my life and my brothers

We ruined Dad's Christmas and we forever emotionally payed for it. After that there was nothing Dad could ever do in the future to win my trust. The curiosity of being a kid did not deserve the severity of that punishment. I began to plot my escape from home at age eleven.

9

Recession

The early 1970's was a heyday for the trucking industry and independent truckers. There was a dramatic rise in the popularity of the trucker culture. Truck drivers were romanticized as modern-day cowboys, bad boys, and outlaws. This was partly due to the CB radios they used to relay information to each other, especially if police were spotted. They were like a bunch of Gladys Kravitz's on the radio. This all suited Dad just fine.

On his CB Dad would say, "breaker-breaker, the fuzz is wearing pantyhose on Hillbilly Highway marker 20." That meant there was a police car in the middle of the divided highway radaring cars and trucks going by at mile marker twenty.

He took that CB radio everywhere he went. We literally did not go anywhere without that radio blasting and driving all of us insane. We had to listen to him rambling on it non-stop from point A to B to C. He even had a six-foot-high portable and flexible antenna mounted on top of the 1967 Ford Country Squire station wagon. He routed the connection wire down the front windshield into the motor and through the dashboard to get the antenna cable connected to the radio.

Dad only had one CB radio so he had to disassemble it from his semi-truck and hook it up in the station wagon every time we went anywhere. By the time he was finished screwing around with it and adjusting all the knobs, which produced high-pitched squeaks and squeals, Mom still wasn't ready to leave the house from trying to get herself and three kids out the door. So, he sat in the car, yacked on the CB and blew the car horn until Mom came out of the house fuming from his impatience.

In 1971, fuel costs started rising and Dad was struggling to make ends meet as an independent truck driver. When he was home, which gradually became more often than not, he stayed in the basement depressed. Then he got more depressed and almost stopped working altogether. The only way Mom could get Dad to work was by going on the road with him, for days and a week at a time, sometimes two, while I was in fifth grade. Mom quit her job at Monkey Wards and started going on long-haul jobs with Dad because he made more money than she did. She didn't make enough to support us.

Since Donna the baby sitter had stuck her rear through the storm window, Mom and Dad believed they were better off without us kids having a babysitter. They couldn't afford to pay for one anyway. Mom prepared all our meals before they left. All I had to do was warm up dinner in the oven, dish it out, and wash and dry the dishes. We ate our usual cereal of Captain Crunch or Sugar Smacks for breakfast and suffered through the school lunches some mystery meat. I woke my brothers up, got them to come downstairs to eat, and made sure Danny did all the things he was supposed to do like wash his face, brush his teeth, and so on. He was eight years old.

The biggest challenge was getting everyone out the door on time so we wouldn't be late for school. When we got home from school, we did our homework, played outside, ate dinner, got a bath, and started the whole thing over again the next day, and the next, and the next.

Our parents called every night from a pay phone to make sure we were OK. There was no way to get back in touch with them. They assured us that we were fine and would be home soon. They didn't know exactly when they would be home because they had to wait on a load to bring back if one wasn't readily available from their drop off point. We were instructed to go next door for help if there was an emergency. Thank God we didn't burn the house down or get into any mischief that we had to answer to. After the Christmas whaling, we knew that staying alive meant not causing any problems that they could find out about.

* * *

In 1972, when I was in sixth grade, Dad and Mom moved us to Wheelersburg, Ohio, affectionately called "The Burg." Wheelersburg sits on the other side of the river from Greenup. The rural region is part of the Appalachian Mountains.

Mom said we needed to move from Lincoln Park because she and Dad were worried that we would get bused to the inner city of Detroit for school. Our house was only two blocks from the elementary school. That's why they moved there in the first place, so we could walk. If we ended up getting bused to the inner city for school, they would be too worried about leaving us for days on end.

By the early 1970's segregation and racial isolation in the North was increasing. Some thought that the only way to end segregation in Detroit was by busing African American students to the Caucasian suburban districts, and busing the mostly white kids to the inner-city schools.

The desegregation effort started in Pontiac, Michigan. Before the school year started in 1971, the Ku Klux Klan used dynamite to blow up ten empty Pontiac school buses that were to be used for busing the kids to different schools. Parents in the suburbs became outraged that their kids would soon be bused to the inner-city schools and began suing the state. A state trial court ordered a desegregation plan including fifty-three school districts involving 780,000 students and requiring at least 310,000 of them to be bused daily on the school days so that each school, each grade, and each classroom would reflect the racial make-up of the entire fifty-three school district area. The suit went up to the Supreme Court.

When the Supreme Court handed down its decision in the summer of 1974, it ruled the Detroit school system, with its 35% white student population, would have to figure out how to desegregate itself without the help of the ring of white suburbs surrounding it because it was not proven that the suburbs had participated in creating the segregation in Detroit.

We didn't have any people of color in our school. I remember my parents talking with other adults about the busing situation, fearing we would be bused to the inner city of Detroit and forced to integrate with black children. The fact is, their community would have been accepting us into their schools, and we would have been fighting to keep them out of ours. Instead of waiting out a decision, my parents moved to the hills of rural white America. As it turned out, the scare in Detroit didn't come to fruition anyway.

Dad wouldn't let us watch television when there were black people on the show like The Jefferson's. It wasn't much different than I Love Lucy or the Carol Burnett shows. He didn't respect bossy women, black people, or anyone different than him. He firmly believed that white men were the boss and everyone else was not. It became clear to me from early on that white men were in control, made and enforced the rules.

On move day from Lincoln Park, Dad and his bar friends placed everything we owned into a U-Haul trailer. Dad pulled it down the road with the Ford Country Squire station wagon. Many things were left behind because we didn't have enough room in the trailer, like the ice skates, skate boards, and bicycles. If you didn't sleep on it, sit on it, or cook with it, it stayed at the curb. I don't know what happened to the bowling and pin ball machines, but they didn't make the priority list.

Somehow, Dennis Jr.'s prize rare coin collection came up missing when we arrived in Wheelersburg. For years he collected rare coins and filled Whitman blue cardboard books with Lincoln cents, Indian

Head cents, Buffalo nickels, Mercury dimes, silver dollars, fifty cent pieces, all with 'S' and 'D' series for years going back to the 1800's. Dennis Jr. didn't ever cry, but when he discovered that his coin collection was missing, he cried hard.

* * *

We moved into a small single wide trailer barely big enough for one person, much less five and a dog. The temporary trailer was home until Mom and Dad could find a house to purchase.

We arrived in Wheelersburg with Spunky, a hyper but precious miniature poodle that my brothers and I adored. Unfortunately, the burden of taking care of Spunky fell on Mom's dime, like feeding and cleaning up his poop, fell on Mom's dime. Between the yipping dog and all of us tightly piled up in the trailer, she flipped over the edge.

Our family ventured out one late afternoon. Dad hooked a chain on Spunky and secured it to the fence outside the trailer. This perplexed us. Spunky, who had baby powdered fur and manicured toe nails, didn't leave the inside of the house. I had a sick feeling in my stomach. I asked, "Why are we leaving Spunky outside, it's getting dark?" No answer.

Later, when the station wagon pulled up in front of the tattered trailer, Spunky had miraculously freed himself from the chain and found himself a new family to take care of him. My brothers and I searched and searched the neighborhood crying until it was too dark to search any longer. Spunky was gone for good and we knew it.

* * *

During the house hunting, Mom and Dad took Dennis Jr. and me to Aunt Fran's and Uncle Scotty's in rural York, Kentucky to stay for a couple weeks before school started. Aunt Fran was Dad's half-sister on his father's side. Her family owned hundreds of acres of land where they cultivated tobacco. They produced a large garden that supplied enough food for a year. Cows, chickens, pigs, and roosters filled the yard. A store was nowhere to be found in that area of the Appalachia. They didn't need one, they lived off the land.

I showed up at Aunt Frans with outfits Mom bought in the suburbs of Detroit all consisting of flowered short shorts, tank tops, and a pixie haircut. Each outfit varied in color but not style. In this area, from what I could witness, girls and women weren't allowed to wear shorts, pants or cut their hair.

Aunt Fran and her family were members of the Pentecostal church. Uncle Scotty was the preacher. Fran's family didn't say a word about my lack of covered clothing or pixie hairdo. They opened their arms and hearts to me and Dennis Jr. They loved having us visit. I deeply treasure the time we enjoyed at Aunt Fran's playing with our cousins.

Every morning Fran cooked a big loving country breakfast with homemade biscuits made from scratch, eggs from the chicken house, bacon, sausage, and many variations of fine jam canned from the previous season of blackberries and strawberries. After breakfast we hoed, helped weed the garden and picked vegetables for the evening meal.

Aunt Fran's convictions prevented her from wearing pants, but she sported Uncle Scotty's britches when she hoed weeds in the tobacco field on hot and humid summer days. Back in the kitchen she donned a to-the-knee hand-made cotton dress and apron. She made all her and the kid's clothes.

Several times during the day Aunt Fran asked us to line up at the back door. Each kid received a big bath towel for the group activity. When she said, "Go", we ran through the house in a single file line gloriously screaming while fanning and waving the towels up and down to shoo the flies out the front door. All the shooing created a massive wind force that even the strongest flies couldn't withstand. We laughed with delight and were told what a good job we did.

Since we ran in and out of the house all day long and let the flies in, it was our job to shew them out, especially before Aunt Fran cooked our country dinner.

Dennis Jr. rode the mule that Uncle Scotty used to plow the fields. I helped out by stringing beans, and shucking corn. The old country house lacked air conditioning. The white box fan on the floor in the kitchen only rattled and stirred the hot air around especially when the oven cooked the biscuits, potatoes and mouthwatering apple and peach pies.

Aunt Fran's family belonged to the Apostolic Pentecostal Church on Big White Oak road in York, Kentucky. They attended service three times a week to listen to Uncle Scotty's sermon. I could only understand every few words that he preached.

He began preaching by taking a deep breath and releasing a minute of sputtered words. Then, gasped and inhaled two or three times in a row with longer and deeper breaths as he extended his head backwards. He gasped and spit out more words that launched flying sweat from his brow. The spit hung in the air and created rainbows above Uncle Scotty's head as it connected with the sun beating through the windows in the hot, stuffy, and humid one room church.

After some time of preaching unfiltered damnation and spitfire hell directed at anyone who committed a sin and not right with the Lord, a fellow Christian would receive the message and connected with the Holy Spirit. They'd stand up in the pew with arms flailing above their heads while praising the Lord God Almighty.

After one got a-goin', many followed by a-wavin' like a Home Comin' Queen with heads a-tiltin' to heaven. The spirit heightened in the pews and the preachin' got louder and louder.

I saw a big hefty woman launch into the church aisle. She ran around the perimeter of the pews several times speaking in tongues before landing in front of the preacher, Uncle Scotty. The spirited woman spun around a few times praising the Lord before crash landing on the floor. She lay in the aisle between the pews and flipped and flopped like a fish out of water. The bottom of her dress extended above her head exposing white cotton briefs a-tuckin' and a-rollin' up to her breasts in the sea of fat.

Usually a curious one and front row observer, I ran into the next to last row of pews and stayed there until things settled down. From then on out, I took cover. I took my seat near the back row, but not the last row just in case the spirted flapped their arms and wacked me while circling the pews.

After a couple weeks visiting Aunt Fran, my brothers and I ventured to Wurtland, Kentucky to spend time with Aunt Bernice and her family. Aunt Bernice was Dad's half-sister on his father's side and full sister to Fran and Thelma.

Aunt Bernice owned and operated a Snyder's Potato Chip route. Snyder's produces pretzels, sandwich crackers, potato chips, cookies, tortilla chips, popcorn, nuts, and lots of other fun snacks.

Dennis Jr., Danny and I rode in the front of the truck and helped Aunt Bernice deliver snacks to her retail customers during half the day of our visit. I loved watching Aunt Bernice operate the box truck and shift gears on the floor while laughing the whole-time telling stories. She let each of us carry boxes of potato chips from the back of the truck to the dock. We enjoyed every second of the working experience while trying every snack offered. I had a glimmer of hope that I could earn money and be my own boss after experiencing Aunt Bernice's success as a woman small business owner.

She sadly passed September 1, 2018 before I got a chance to visit her. She's home with the Lord.

10

Burg

On my first day of school in sixth grade at Wheelersburg Elementary School I wore purple patterned pants and a yellow shirt with stripes. I picked out a few new outfits from a department store before we left Michigan. I loved my stylish new look with all the hippie colors of the 70's.

When Mom took us into the office to register for classes the admissions clerk looked at me like I was a Martian. She politely told Mom that I could go to classes that day but the next day I had to wear a dress or skirt to school and wouldn't be allowed back into the school wearing pants.

In Lincoln Park I wore pants, t-shirts and shorts to school. I didn't own a skirt or dress. The last pink dress and patent leather shoes were worn to church for Easter in first grade. That dress got caked with dirt and mud from playing kick ball in granny's yard after church service.

The admissions clerk instructed Mom to get Dennis Jr's hair cut because boys were required to wear their hair above their ears and above their collar in the back, just like in the military. He couldn't come back to school either until he got his hair in proper order.

It was 1972 and long hair was all the rage. It was a fashion that filtered down the social pyramid from upper-middle-class hippies to ordinary working men and boys, but not in this part of the Bible belt and not at our elementary school. Dennis Jr. refused to get the top of his hair cut but the back and sides were in line with the militant rules.

We weren't poor, but we didn't have any money. Mom took me to Rinks department store to buy some different school outfits, something appropriate for the antiquated rules of this elementary school. Mom paid on credit.

Defunct Rinks was a low-end bargain basement store, a cross between Walmart and Value City, and the only available option to shop unless we went into Portsmouth, Ohio. People with money drove two hours north to Columbus to buy school clothes, but many without money, like us, shopped for clothes at Rinks.

Quite a few people wore the same outfits to school. I was mortified to see other girls wearing my new dress on day two. Mom had always made sure we dressed in style and had good quality clothes to wear. When she washed an article of clothing from Rinks, the all the colors faded into each other and produced a tie-dye effect. You definitely couldn't wash your white underwear with colored clothes or they would come out ugly gray or blotched pink.

Dad and Mom found a nice three-bedroom brick ranch house at the top of a long hill on Filmore Lane in Wheelersburg, next to the high school. Dad and Mom purchased the house from Hearst "Skip" and Sybil Meadows on a seller financed land contract because we didn't have the money for a down payment or jobs to even make the first payment. The Meadows' saw something good in our family and offered to help.

Skip was the choir director at a local Baptist church and asked our family to join them for Sunday service. I accepted the offer, but the rest of the family declined. They picked me up on many Sunday mornings to attend Sunday school and the morning church service. I will always be grateful for Skip's kindness and generosity. He sang like an angel. I needed an angel in my life. They were kind enough to not kick us out of their house while we counted change in tin cans to make the late mortgage payments each month.

I was trying to make new friends at school but felt like an outsider until I was approached by a neighbor girl that hung out with a group of girls that seemed to be longtime friends. If you were accepted into their clique you had an instant group of friends. They were smart and appeared to be in the popular crowd. In Lincoln Park, all the kids were my friends. We didn't have to pick a group to associate with. In my small rural school, you didn't pick your friends, they picked you.

Mom signed my brothers and me up to get free school lunches while she and Dad looked for work. I believed that associating with this new group of friends would not work out for me if I was getting free lunches. When in front of the cash register at the school cafeteria, you either paid a quarter for lunch or yelled out "FREE!"

Those who yelled "FREE!" had to blast it out so everyone in the cafeteria could hear them admit to their given social status. If the poor student was meek, the cash register lady, an overweight oily haired woman sitting on a decrepit wooded stool ready to collapse, would force it out of them by saying, "What did you say!!?" The kid would have to repeat the embarrassing four-letter word again. Yelling "FREE!" was another way of saying "I'm free of ever having friends that aren't dirt poor."

"Freeloaders" were looked down upon and made fun of by the in-crowd. There seemed to be a lot of pretentious people in Wheelersburg compared to other places we lived. So, I either didn't eat lunch or took a quarter out of Mom's tin cans to pay for my meal. I figured I would pay her back somehow, someday. When we came up short on paying the mortgage payment, I would just not eat lunch.

* * *

Moving from the suburb of a big city to Wheelersburg proved to be devastating on the economic front for our family in 1972. Richard Nixon was President of the United States and the Vietnam War was in full force. The 1970's recession was a period of economic stagnation in much of the Western world, putting an end to the overall Post World War II economic expansion.

It differed from many previous recessions because high unemployment and high inflation existed simultaneously. Beginning in 1972, motorists faced long lines at gas stations. The 1970s oil crisis knocked the wind out of the global economy and helped trigger a stock market crash, soaring inflation, and high unemployment.

Responding to the crisis, the U.S. federal government began to ration oil and gas and imposed a nationwide 55 mph speed limit on all highways and interstates to promote fuel conservancy. The fuel crisis and subsequent rationing caused gas prices to skyrocket. Independent truckers, like Dad, needed low fuel costs and the ability to drive above 55 mph. Profit margins were low for truckers. They needed to pull more loads per week to make ends meet and these restrictions slowed them down.

Hillbilly Highway was full of weigh stations to trap and fine owner-operators for carrying too much weight on their trailers. Many truckers struggled to feed their families. Truckers found ways to sneak around the weigh stations like they did on EK road in front of granny's house.

Truckers got paid by the mile and it was worth it to dodge the "fuzz" and maneuver through the back roads of the hills with dangerous curves like Dad did. An eighteen-wheeler hauling gas could jack-knife and light up the whole county if it exploded by going too fast around dangerous curves. Dad said' "New truckers only got one chance to go slow on switchbacks or they'll lay that big rig down and burn to holly hell."

For Dad, the cut-throughs usually added an hour to the time it took to get to the highway, but they eliminated fines, and that was important. Dad took pride in his driving skills of hauling gas all over the United States without having a single accident. He'd say, "It takes one-time a-goin' too fast to get lit up."

Dad kept on trucking when he could get loads as an independent owner-operator. Trucking was the only job he knew well. He enjoyed being a renegade truck driver and, on the road, away from home. After we settled into the new house, Mom started driving with him again, leaving us for days or a week or two at a time.

* * *

Entering sixth grade in a new school was exciting and challenging for me. One of my teachers, Mr. Gary Hiembach, who became assistant principal of Wheelersburg Elementary School the next year, noticed that I had potential to become a good student. We both had strawberry-blonde hair and instantly formed a bond because of our hair color. Mr. Hiembach called on me in class and challenged me to start thinking before responding. Mr. Hiembach demonstrated faith in me and provided encouragement for me to work hard. He wanted me to succeed and that support alone gave me confidence to believe in myself.

In seventh grade, I took a Manual Dexterity Test with the rest of the kids in my grade. I moved washers from one post to the next. I was told how they couldn't believe how fast and accurate I was on all parts of the test – better than anyone they had ever seen come through the school. I looked around and saw others dropping washers and fumbling with the tweezers used to move the washers. But, when the written report came out, I was told that I would make a good secretary, truck driver, or factory worker. This revelation made me feel sick to the bone.

Granny was right, I knew too much for one but not enough for two. I didn't tell anyone. My girlfriends were bragging about becoming doctors, lawyers, scientists, and teachers. I didn't get that on my report and couldn't figure out why not. I made the same grades in all subjects, if not better than my friends, all A's and an occasional B. What had happened? I was upset and humiliated. Becoming a secretary was not what I had in mind. It certainly wouldn't earn me enough money to be independent. Women weren't independent if they had to be secretaries and take orders from men. Why couldn't women be the bosses?

The brand of milk we used came in cartons that had a picture of a cow named "Bossy." I liked to boss my brothers around, so they called me "Bossy the Cow." The name stuck with me for a while when I tried to assert authority on them. I was going to be the boss, even if I was only the boss of myself. Secretaries and line workers didn't have boss titles and I had already had enough of the ups and downs of truck driving in my life. My new mission became crystal clear after the results of the test. I "knew too much for one and not enough for two." I needed to work harder at school to make up the difference.

I began carrying my entire set of school books home every day even if I didn't have any homework assignments. As long as I made good grades I could sign up for the tougher courses. I began to develop a lifelong passion for learning. I read and read and read everything I could get my hands on, including many books I checked out of the public library. I signed up for the classes that my new friends were taking, the ones that were needed to prepare for college.

I didn't have anyone to mentor me, but Mom and Dad encouraged me to do well in school. I wasn't sure exactly what college was but I was determined to go.

I fit in with the established group of nine close friends, all girls. The boys didn't have any interest in me and I didn't give them a thought either. I was too busy studying, reading books, and playing basketball with anyone who would play me.

On birthday weekends our group of friends took turns having slumber parties at each of our houses. When it was my turn to host a birthday party my stomach churned. I asked Mom and she said, "Go ask your father." I asked Dad and he said, "Go ask your mother."

After several attempts they finally succumbed to the idea of having teenage girls over for slumber party during which there would be no slumbering, not for anyone in the house. I had hoped that Mom and Dad would not say "yes" but I felt obligated to host since I was so kindly invited to all their parties.

I wanted to have my friends over but feared that my dad would come home drunk and embarrass me. He did, but not enough to ruin the party. We had an amazing time bringing back the dead, including our late music teacher, in a seance. We also took turns lifting our bodies one at a time above our heads from the floor. One girl would lie on the floor and the others would circle around her and place only two fingers under her body. I'll never be sure how we managed to lift 120 pounds of dead weight with two fingers each from ten teenage girls, but we had fun doing it.

* * *

Mom saved up enough money for my brothers and me to go to the Porter Township community pool during the summers of seventh and eighth grade. It cost $250 for a family membership each year and took every dime she had to make this sacrifice so we could spend summers enjoying our friends and have a place to go while Mom and Dad trucked the highways.

Dad came to the pool one time and stood at the high dive with Danny. Dad coaxed and coaxed him until he finally climbed the fifteen feet of stairs and walked to the end of the plank. He just stood there looking over the edge of the board with intense fear. After more prompting, he got the courage to jump. When he leaped his tiny frame spun forward. He landed like a brick smack dap on this face and stomach. The pressure of the water from the fall just about knocked his front teeth out. He had dental problems for years after the face dive.

＊＊

When we moved to the rural region, I struggled with how to fit into the culture. There was nothing progressive about this area. I had played T-Ball, field hockey, and flag football on a girls' team in Lincoln Park and was always in the starting lineup and first pick on any pickup team. This new school didn't have any sports teams for girls in sixth through eighth grades. The only sports team available for girls was track that began in ninth grade. The boys had many sports teams that started in sixth grade.

Dad put up a basketball pole in the driveway when we arrived at our new house. It still stands forty-five years later. I either played basketball or rode my bike up and down the hills for miles when I wasn't studying or at a friend's house.

Our school had a dance for eighth grade boys and girls. All my friends were asked pretty quickly to the dance, but not me. I was a tom-boy and boys didn't know what to think of me. When any boy came to our house to see Dennis Jr., I challenged them to a basketball game. I usually beat them and they didn't seem to like that.

Finally, cute little Scotty Green got the courage to ask me to the dance. I was one of the few girls left to choose from. Girls were not allowed to ask boys to the dance and it was unacceptable to go without a date. Scotty was a head below my height.

I didn't want to go because I had to wear a dress, but I accepted anyway. Mom and Dad couldn't afford to buy me a dress so Mom got a neighbor to make me one from a pattern she picked out. The cotton flowered dress started at the top of my chin with scratchy lace and ended at the floor, a look straight out of the 1800's. As if the dress wasn't bad enough, I had to wear a scratchy slip under it too. God help the person who could see your legs through the dress inside a dark school dance floor in the gym if you didn't have on a slip. A spot light might just shine on your ass for all to see your figure. The two items were deemed inseparable and protesting and objecting was not an option. I felt like fish out of water inside a sack of potatoes.

Mom and I shopped at Rinks discount department store and purchased a pair of platform sandals that put me another six inches above Scotty Green. We put our hands on each other's shoulders and kept the mandatory two feet of separation while dancing. After the dance my hips hurt for a week from rocking back and forth on the platform shoes.

The next day I was back in my weekend 70's hot pants and home-made Raggedy Ann and Raggedy Andy halter top that I made with from a pattern and sewed together on Mom's machine. I started learning how to sew in seventh grade. Home Economics was a required course for girls in rural schools and I actually loved learning how to sew and bake. I am thankful to have learned those skills in school.

The boys were required to take "Shop" and make things out of wood. Dennis Jr. surprised me at Christmas one year with a beautiful jewelry box that he made for me. I will treasure that unconditional act of love from him for the rest of my life.

* * *

My school didn't spare the rod. It's no wonder domestic violence was never talked about. Whoopin's were common at school. The Shop teacher was called into the hall when an infraction occurred with one of the students and a paddle was used for punishment. During that time, we didn't get sent to the principal's office for behaving disrespectfully. We just got licked.

My infractions involved not being able to keep quiet. Unless we were seated alphabetically, I always sat in the front row because I didn't want to miss out on anything the teacher said and it helped me pay attention. But there were times of boredom. I'd turn around to talk to the person behind me while the teacher was lecturing. I got sent out into the hall to receive the corporal punishment administered by the Shop teacher with a long wooden paddle that had small holes in it to add extra sting.

A single infraction got me or any other student three hard licks. I had to spread my legs wide, bend over at the waist, put my arms straight out with only a bending of the wrist against the locker. The licks were so loud that they echoed throughout the halls for all students in the school to hear as a reminder that they better follow the rules or get licked.

If you made any noise you got another lick. There were no negotiations in the hallway. You just shut up and took your licks. You'd think with the beatings at home that I could keep my mouth shut in school. I didn't get many of these paddling's, but one was too many in my opinion. I didn't and don't believe in physical abuse in any form.

After a couple times of getting licks, I told the Shop teacher that I was on my period that he could not hit me with the board or blood would squirt everywhere. His face looked shocked. He left to get a woman teacher and they discussed it. Apparently, this remark spread among the teachers because I never got marshalled to the hall again for a lickin'. I tried to keep quiet and pay attention, but not always.

* * *

First Year for Girls Basketball

In addition to volleyball, basketball was introduced into the girls athletic program this year at WHS. The girls were coached by Miss Janet Stone and Mr. Randy Parker.

The team practiced hard after a late start, and even though their first season was not successful, the girls commented they were looking forward to having a better record next year.

During tournament play the girls showed much improvement by playing a tough game against Northwest. They were defeated by only one point.

Teri Darnell uses good offense as she dribbles down court.

The team displays its spirit as they gather in a huddle.

In the summer of 1972, sixth grade, Title IX of the education amendments of 1972 was enacted into law. Title IX prohibits federally funded educational institutions from discriminating against students or employees based on sex. As a result of Title IX any school that receives any federal money from elementary to university level must provide fair and equal treatment of the sexes in all areas, including athletics.

Before Title IX few opportunities existed for female athletes. Facilities, supplies, and funding were severely lacking at my school in Wheelersburg, Ohio. Title IX was designed to correct those imbalances. Women's and men's programs were required to devote the same resources to locker rooms, medical treatment, training, coaching, practice times, travel and per diem allowances, equipment, practice facilities, tutoring and recruitment.

Since the enactment of Title IX, women's participation in sports has grown exponentially. In high school the number of girl athletes increased from just 295,000 in 1972 to more than 2.6 million in 2018. And, Title IX decreases the dropout rate of girls from high school and increases the number of women who pursue higher education and complete college degrees.

Rural Wheelersburg wasn't in any hurry to obey the new law. I didn't know anything about Title IX until the end of ninth grade, almost four years after enactment of the law. We suddenly got a volleyball, basketball, and softball team for girls in my sophomore year in high school. In ninth grade we could only play half-court basketball after school in a program called The Girl's Athletic Association (GAA). We were called "Feminine Intramuralists."

Six-player girls' basketball (called "half-court") looks like two separate three-on-three games played at the same time on the same court during the intramural games. No one could cross the midcourt line. Players were limited to two dribbles. An "official" ran the ball up the court after a basket was made. Eventually "half-court" basketball faded by the wayside as females demanded to be on equal playing fields with males and allowed to play by the same game rules.

With Title IX, we were allowed to go into the boy's locker room to lift weights on a restricted schedule as long as we did not interfere with their program. The weights didn't get moved into a shared location as long as I attended the school. I lifted weights with enthusiasm, trying to add muscle to the bones of my skinny body. I was 5'6" and only weighed 105 pounds from running so many miles in track and to maintain my sanity.

Starting in my freshman year of high school I ran the mile race in track and usually won. Before Title IX our school gym clothes were used as our track uniforms. After Title IX they were replaced with polyester uniforms that had numbers to identify the players. Like the boys' teams, we traveled to other schools to play sports.

Playing sports changed my life. Discipline became a natural part of me when I started playing sports. It allowed me to develop better and healthier relationships with other people. Our coaches were our mentors and provided a positive outlook and hope for all of us. Playing sports trained my mind to think clearly and find new strategies to deal with problems while remaining calm. I had enough problems to deal with at home and playing on a team kept me focused in a healthy direction.

The interactions with other players on my teams, opponents and coaches helped prepare me for all the diversity in my life. By participating in sports, I developed leadership skills and learned how to set goals that were difficult to reach, to stretch myself, to try harder and go further. My gracious appreciation goes to all the courageous people who had the foresight to give girls like me a chance, like Billy Jean King, Patsy T. Mink, Birch Bayh, Nancy Hogshead-Makar, and President Richard Nixon who signed Title IX into law. Thank you from the bottom of my heart.

In Wheelersburg, high school boy's football and basketball wove the community together. The after-school students, including me, decorated the school halls with signs like "Burg's the Word" and "Go Pirates" a couple days before each game. We filled every square inch of the halls with balloons, banners, and orange and black crepe paper streaming from the ceiling.

Every adult and student in "The Burg" ventured to the games for a night of rip-roaring excitement with mostly wins and an occasional agony of defeat. Every play of the game was talked about for days until it was time to get ready for the next one. The male athletes were treated like gods and could do no wrong. When the girl's team ramped up for basketball the crowd was just as rowdy and the stands were filled with patrons. Wheelersburg people love their athletic teams and supported the girls too, after we finally got a chance to get started.

11

Changes

As the price of diesel fuel shot up, Dad's demeanor cascaded downward. Mom put on a pants suit purchased in Detroit and applied for a job at Montgomery Wards in Portsmouth, Ohio. Monkey Wards could only offer Mom the minimum wage of $1.60 per hour for her experience as a telephone debt collector. In Lincoln Park she had earned three times that rate. Mom needed more than minimum wage to pay the mortgage and feed us. She took a waitress job at the Stone Pipe Inn, a steak and seafood fine dining restaurant in Portsmouth, thirty minutes away.

Mom worked the dinner shift hoping to get good tips to supplement her minimum wage hourly rate. She left home at 4 p.m. and returned at 2 a.m. most nights of the week. Since Mom's left leg is three inches shorter than her right from the grafting surgery after the first accident as a child, she experiences constant pain when walking.

She places all her weight on the ball of her right foot with each stride. Her ankle doesn't flex and it's difficult for her to walk at a normal pace or for an extended period of time. To help her last a whole shift standing on her leg while waitressing, she stuffed a Kotex in the back of her shoe so she could put weight on her heel.

Mom's physical condition and intellect suited her for an office job but none existed in this rural Bible belt area, especially for an exodus of Kentucky and an implant from Michigan. Even her southern accent and being raised across the Ohio River in Greenup didn't help her get a leg up on a job. Good jobs were given to employee's relatives who planned to stay in the area.

Mom was a transient looking for a better life for her family and nobody opened a door for her to have one. Mom's survivalist attitude and resilience kept us alive. The pennies, nickels, dimes, quarters, fifty cent pieces, and occasional silver dollars collected in waitress tips were placed in coffee cans on the shelf in the laundry room to pay for the mortgage and utilities needed to own a house, her American Dream.

At the end of the month, Mom took the cans off the shelf and placed them on the kitchen table. My brothers and I helped her count and stuff the coins into tubular paper wrappers that she deposited at the bank. If Dad didn't have a good month of trucking, we could tell at the end of the count that she would be short on paying the bills. She didn't say a word but the air became thick as her shoulders slumped in despair.

In 1974, Dennis Jr., an industrious and a hard worker found a summer job at Bihl's farm. He didn't have any desire to attend college. He was an outdoors guy. He got a job picking vegetables because Mom and Dad didn't have any extra cash to give him, for anything.

Dennis Jr. walked two miles to work from our house to Lick-Run-Lyra Bloom Road where Bihl's Farm was located. The long dirt road sprouted rows and rows of corn in fields spanning for as long as the eye can see.

I was a competitive mile runner on the girl's track team, and I ran my seven-mile long-distance training route on Lick-Run-Lyra and Gleim Road during high school practices and on the weekend. The route took me past Memorial Burial Park, a massive cemetery on this desolate road. I increased my long-distance minute per mile from seven to six through the section that passes the cemetery. When the wind howled and blew the corn stalks from side-to-side, I felt the spirts in the cemetery coming alive and was afraid that one would get me. When I first started this training route, my coach Ms. Stone followed me on her bicycle to make sure it was safe. She said she believed the route was fine for a fifteen-year-old girl with long flowing strawberry-blonde hair, but even back then I wondered.

Dennis Jr. bought a used orange 1972 Yamaha 125 Enduro for transportation to work. He purchased the motorcycle from farm money and his early morning paper route. He taught me how to ride it around our neighborhood.

In 1975 at age fifteen I got a summer job on Bihl's Farm too. Dennis Jr. drove me back and forth to work on the back seat of his motorcycle. We hit pot holes and bounced up and down the dusty gravel road laughing and having a great time.

Left-Right-Left

I picked strawberries in the field with other high school kids and anyone else the farm could get to work for minimum wage or less, like migrant workers. To get started we were handed time cards. I punched the card into a mechanical time clock by inserting the heavy paper card into a slot. When the time card hit a contact at the rear of the slot the machine, it printed the day and time stamp on the card. That's how our hours were tracked for calculating pay.

The girls picked strawberries and the boys picked heavier vegetables. Each picker was assigned a row. On my dirt row I picked half the plants that faced the path and worked my way down to the end of the row. I switched rows to my back-side for the return picking. The rows were a quarter mile long.

For the person working opposite of me on a row, I tried to be respectful and not encroach on their space while picking the bushes clean. I ate a few big juicy ripe strawberries along the way. If a berry was green, I left it on the vine for a later time when the fields opened for the U-pick your own strawberries customers.

I quickly learned by observing that my picking method of stooping took too long. The migrant worker in front of me was half way down the row as I got my rear end up and down off the ground from digging around in the first couple of plants for strawberries.

The most efficient and effective picking method was to bend at the waist, keep your legs straight, and let your arms dangle through the bushes to get to all the strawberries. Standing up to pick strawberries required extra effort. Instead, I bent, dangled, and slid sideways down the rows for four hours a day during the hot humid summer. I sported a dark tan on one side of my body. The other side was still pasty white as you would expect from a red-head.

I earned $1.25 an hour plus an extra ten cents for each flat of strawberries picked if I filled more than eight flats in an hour. I was usually able to bust the quota and pick two extra flats in an hour. According to my Social Security Statement, I made $214 that summer. At $1.45 an hour, including the twenty-cent bonus, I worked thirty-six half days in the summer of 1975.

I wanted to go to basketball camp for a week during high school break. The camp was at Ohio University in Athens, Ohio. It cost $200 (almost $1,000 in today's dollars). The cost included staying in a dorm room, food, and daily basketball instruction by the University's head coach.

The only way I could figure out how to get to camp was to earn money picking strawberries on the farm, and I did it. The University experience opened my eyes to a whole new world. Students came from all over the state to attend the prestigious camp.

It didn't matter what race you were or what your socio-economic status was, we were all treated the same and with respect. What did matter was how hard you worked and how well you got along with the other girls. Teamwork was preached by the coach.

Having the camp experience cemented my desire to go to college. Visiting a college gave me a real picture to go with my dream. I began to believe that getting a college degree was attainable with hard work.

**

Julie, Lori, and Jan were my closest high school friends and lived close by. Julie lived a couple houses down from my family. Lori and Jan lived at the bottom of the hill. During Halloween we'd go trick-or-treating together and come home with pillow cases full of candy. At age thirteen Julie, Lori and I ventured out the night before Halloween (Devil's night) to get into mischief. The mischief usually included toilet papering someone's house or soaping their home picture window.

We had a special treat for the neighbors on Devil's night. Our house was located near a corn field. Days ahead of Devil's night we scoured the corn field and brought home dozens of ears of cow corn. We picked the corn that had white moldy stuff on top so it wouldn't be like we were stealing because the top of the corn was rotten. That's what we told ourselves. My parents didn't question our motives.

It was common practice for kids in our area to create a plan for Devil's night. The plan was to 'borrow' cow corn, shuck the corn off the cob until our hands were raw and fill a pillow case with enough corn that you can still carry the sack over your shoulder while running away from the scene of the crime.

When it got dark, we set foot through the neighborhood evaluating our targets for "corning." We wanted neighbors to be home so they could experience the joy of Devil's night too. If we saw a light on inside the house, we'd run up as close as we could and hide in a bush or behind a tree and then throw the corn at the picture window.

The corn hit the glass producing a loud ratty-tat-tat sound. We laughed and laughed and ran to the next house. I don't know how we came up with the idea but we decided to corn cars driving by at the bottom of the hill on busy Gallia Pike road. We didn't think that this would scare the shit out of them, but it did.

An old man chased us down the road in his car after we corned it. We ran through a back yard trying to out maneuver him. It was pitch dark and I couldn't see a thing in front of me. When I got to the bottom of the hill something hard grabbed me around the throat and took me to the ground. A few seconds later, I heard a thump and then an unknown body landed on top of me, it was Julie. Lori didn't follow our path of hanging.

While lying on the ground looking up at the moon light, we realized that we had run into a clothes line. We laughed so hard that we just about wet our pants. I had a ring slice around my throat for a week and Julie had one just under her nose since I was a bit taller than her. We still laughed about this night forty years later at our high school reunion.

* * *

Dennis Jr. had a friend whom I will call Mat. Mat liked to come to our house often. Occasionally we'd play a round of HORSE. I wasn't interested in him any more than he was interested in me for becoming boyfriend and girlfriend. If fact, he would tell me that I wasn't as pretty as my girlfriends and asked me to fix him up with one of them. He wanted to know why I didn't wear makeup. I asked him why he didn't wear it either.

He began doing crazy things when my parents were gone, and they were gone a lot, days and a week at a time when Dad got a load to haul somewhere in the United States. I was fifteen. He was sixteen.

Mat did several strange and disgusting things to get a reaction out of me. He would stand on his head against the dining room wall with his penis hanging out of his pants. When I'd come around the corner and see him upside down with his penis sticking out like a peg on a coat rack I would shriek and run to my room, slam the door, block it with a chair, and wait for him to leave.

I was shocked and ashamed to see his penis. It seemed to always stay bulged out of his pants or shorts. He constantly said that he had a "boner" and needed it sucked and wanted me to do it. I told him that I wouldn't touch him with a ten-foot pole, not ever, but that didn't stop him from continuously trying to get me to suck his dick. I kept telling him to leave me alone or I would tell my parents. He was in heat and wouldn't stop. Every time he came to the house, he'd pull out his penis wanting me to look at it as he jerked it up and down. I'd shriek and run away.

One fall when I was sixteen, I was outside playing basketball. I missed the rim and the ball rolled down the long hill behind our house into the gully. Suddenly someone grabbed me from behind, pulled me tight around my arms and waist, shoved his hard dick between my legs and began humping my rear end with my shorts on like a dog. When he tried to rip off my thin nylon running shorts I broke loose. This same boy had his jeans unbuttoned, unzipped, and half way down his thighs. He stood there with his dick sticking out like a flag on a pole as I turned and ran up the hill, into the house, and into my bedroom, terrified that I could have been raped.

I don't believe it would have mattered if I was a sheep; this teen aged boy full of raging sex hormones was desperate to find a hole to screw. I know I'm not unique. How many other sisters are getting sexually assaulted by their brother's friend who can't keep his penis in his pants? One is too many.

**

One afternoon in tenth grade before I left the house Dad told me to be home before dark. I was about a mile and a half away at Lori's house. The road to her house was a mile downhill from ours. I lost track of time and noticed the sun starting to set. I got on my bicycle and began my journey home. I peddled as fast as I could all the way up the steep hill without stopping to get off my bike and push the last quarter of a mile where the road was straight up and down. I made it the whole way huffing and puffing as my lungs were exploding and thighs burning on fire.

Dusk lingered in the air when I arrived home. Dad was in the house waiting for me. He said, "I told ya to be home before dark." I said, "I made it home before dark. It's dusk." I had pushed it too close and that made him mad. Dusk was dark and that was that. For me dusk still had light. It was the story of our relationship. If I saw white, he saw black. Mom was at work waitressing. He beat me half to death with his belt for coming home from a friend's house at dusk.

I felt like I got set up. I believed that he thought he could start uncontrollably beating me like he beat Mom. This was an unconscionable act of power and control. He took me into his bedroom and beat me as I screamed bloody murder while he yelled at me to obey him from now on. He stopped when I said that I would.

I was falsely accused and received severe punishment for crossing a boundary that was not clearly defined. I was a good teenager, made great grades, excelled at sports, didn't get into any trouble, helped Mom around the house with most chores, helped my brothers with their school work or did it for them, was the caretaker when they went trucking for days and weeks, what more could he ask? This inhumane beating turned my life around for the worse. I hated Dad with every single breath that I inhaled.

* * *

As a sophomore in high school I began to feel sorry for myself. I started making friends with the high school seniors that I met on Bihl's farm that summer and left my pack of sophomores behind. I started drinking like Dad but for me it was a way to relieve the pain of his wrath. I didn't realize at the time that drinking was a result of letting him control me. His unconscionable abuse caused me to go low and drink to escape my thoughts. I wasn't strong enough to go high, not yet.

* * *

On some weekends when Mom was waitressing at the Stone Pipe Inn, Dad made my brothers and I go way out in the sticks with him to his first cousin's house trailer so he could play poker with Bobby and his teenage daughters.

Bobby had multiple sclerosis and was bound to a wheelchair with limited muscular functionality and speech. Until way after midnight Dad drank beer and shots of moonshine, got drunk and attempted to drive us home. He wouldn't let Dennis Jr. or me drive. This became a common weekend occurrence while Mom was working.

On one occasion Dad borrowed another Cousin Gerald's motorcycle. Gerald (pictured above) lived in Dad's home county of

Left-Right-Left 169

Greenup. When we visited with granny, Gerald was the guy Dad snuck off with to drink and raise hell in Ironton. Dad was visiting relatives alright.

Gerald had a reputation for being a real bad boy. He and Dad hung out in Ironton at T&H Grill (Tug & Hug) with Step & a-half, a supposedly beautiful prostitute with a limp. Dad partook in T&H and probably Step & a-half a couple weekends a month. The story goes that Step & a-half was friends with another prostitute named Sharon.

One night, Dad made me ride with him on the back of Gerald's motorcycle to visit Cousin Bobby's trailer. Around midnight I went to the basement of the trailer looking for a place to lie down and get some sleep. I saw Dad exiting the bedroom of one of the teenage girls while zipping up his fly. She followed right behind him. I wanted to vomit.

He looked me in the eye when he saw me and kept walking without saying a word. He was definitely playing poke her.

Later that night he got drunk again and forced me to get on the back of the motorcycle as I pleaded for us to stay there until morning. After the last beating I was afraid of him and what could possible happen to me if I refused to get on the motorcycle, especially since I had just witnessed another sign of his short comings. I believed we would not make it home.

Instead of going home he weaved us down the road, swerving around oncoming traffic, until we arrived at Mom's work, an hour from Cousin Bobby's trailer. He wanted to make sure she was working and not off with some other man, as he frequently accused her of doing instead of working.

He went inside to make sure she was in there. Once satisfied that she wasn't out screwing someone like he had just done with a seventeen-year-old girl with a father who wasn't capable of going down the basement steps to protect her, we managed to get home alive. I wanted to run away from home but I couldn't figure out where to go and I didn't have any money.

12

Confusion

Times were a-changing at Wheelersburg high school. Barry Manilow's "Could It Be Magic" and "I Write the Songs" were replaced "Disco." Songs like "That's the Way You Like It" and "Get Down Tonight" by KC and the Sunshine Band played on the radio. Dance songs such as "Watergate," the "Hustle," and the "Bus Stop," were big hits on the dance floor.

Girl's hair started getting shorter and boy's hair longer. The picture of the year was "One Flew Over the Cuckoo's Nest." I was living crazy times, with a crazy person, and it was my time to break out of my little goody-two-shoes shell. I was sixteen and began to raise hell. This destruction lasted about four months until we moved again.

I befriended a senior with a yellow Volkswagen bug. She lived in our neighborhood. She'd pick me up and we'd go to the liquor store a few miles away. When we went to pay the old man behind the counter, he looked to make sure nobody else was in the store. He'd hurriedly sell us a six pack of Hudepohl-Schoenling Little King Cream Ale beers. We bought Little Kings because they had high alcohol content and not a lot of liquid. I didn't like the taste of beer. I just wanted to numb my brain.

Occasionally, we'd get Boone's Farm Strawberry Hill wine instead of beer. It tasted nasty too. We searched for a place to drink alcohol without driving all the gas out of the car. We usually met up with other teenagers in a field down a curvy dusty road where there was always a bonfire with plenty of alcohol and drugs. At least I had enough sense to not do drugs.

On one ride home through the curvy road I puked all over the inside of her cute little yellow bug. I knew then that I better get a grip on my life or I would end up just like my dad or dead or both. It was time to shift gears.

***

Mom was getting beat on a regular basis when she got home from waitressing. Dad waited up for her to get home. He'd get back to the house about an hour earlier than her after getting drunk in Portsmouth or Ironton with his cousin Gerald. He always accused Mom of cheating on him soon after she walked in the door.

She'd carry her purse full of change into the house and dump it into the empty coffee cans. Then the accusations began and quickly escalated into yelling, shoving, pushing, slapping, kicking her deformed leg, fist punching her body, hair pulling, objects flying in the air, holes in walls, furniture moving, and intense screaming and crying.

On occasional weekends when Mom didn't have to work, she drove my brothers and me to Portsmouth. She sent us into one bar at a time until we found Dad while she stayed in the car. When we located him, he refused to leave the bar. He enjoyed the company of his friends and the bar women more than he cared about being home with us.

We ran in and out of the bar telling Mom that he wouldn't come out. He told us to "git home." Like a dog. We waited for hours sitting inside or standing outside of the car, sometimes in the rain, sometimes in the snow, and sometimes we would just drive back home, usually without him. I could never understand what this search and rescue mission was supposed to accomplish. It always ended in disaster one way or another.

* * *

Dad kept trying to get work as an independent truck driver, but he was having a hard time getting loads of steel or gas to haul because of the recession. He couldn't keep up with the necessary expenses of maintaining the semi-truck either.

When Dad hauled trailer loads of gas for another company as an independent truck driver, he needed some tread on the tires or it wouldn't be safe to take the load. Mom and Dad were stuck in a pickle because they didn't have the money to buy new tires for the semi. He pushed his luck with the ones he had on the truck. He talked with Mom about putting retreads on the tires. I didn't know what a retread was but apparently you can wrap rubber around a tire to make it go further when the tread wears down.

When Dad did get work, he would come home and have both of my brothers help him wash the truck, tear it apart and put it back together with a bunch of wrenches and grease. Parts were placed in several coffee cans and buckets full of gasoline so the parts could soak. They'd take old tooth brushes and clean the parts in the gas filled containers.

I witnessed Dad and my brothers practically bathing in the gasoline when they were finished for the evening trying to get the grease off their hands and under their fingernails. When they needed more clean gas, they'd take a garden hose, stick it in the gas tank of the station wagon, suck on the hose until gas spewed into their mouths, place the hose in a red steel gas can then spit the gas out of their mouths onto the driveway.

After some practice it was rare for them to get gas in their mouths. They learned how to bend the hose right before the gas shot to the end. With the pressure in the hose it poured nicely into the can when they straightened the kink in the hose out.

Dennis Jr. got a lot of practice at this process when filling up the tank of his Yamaha 125 Enduro from the gas in the station wagon. The motorcycle didn't have a license plate so he only drove it on back roads. Gas stations didn't exist on the back roads. In fact, there was only one gas station in town and it was on the main road near the police station.

* * *

Dad decided that he was good at fixing Televisions so he opened a TV Repair shop in Greenup. No, not in Wheelersburg, close to home where there were more people per square mile that owned TVs. His TV repair business in Greenup gave him an excuse to go through Portsmouth, where all his favorite bars and women were located. He had to drive through Portsmouth to get to Greenup. His plan had enough merit that Mom fell for it.

Dad could fix just about anything and taught me to do the same. He spent all the family savings renting a small store front on the town square and purchasing TV tubes of every kind, but there just weren't enough TVs in Greenup that needed repair.

Mom told me that after his failed business attempt, he tried to shoot himself inside our garage, where his small workshop was located. I didn't know about this until many years later. I wasn't home when the shotgun went off. Fortunately, he missed another attempt at dying.

A time before, Dad took my brothers and me to a car race on a dirt track. At the end of the race he asked some guy if he could take a short ride on his motorcycle. We were shocked when we saw Dad take the bike on the race track. He got it up to speed as fast as it could go. Instead of turning the bike when approaching the curve, he went straight and under the bleachers. He took out several two by fours as they broke across his chest. Finally, one knocked him off the bike. He laid there until we ran over to where he crashed thinking he was dead. He got up stumbling and said for us to go get in the car. He drove to the first local bar and finished getting drunk. He told the suicide attempt story to anyone in the bar that would listen. They felt sorry for him and bought him more drinks.

After the TV repair venture ended, one morning I woke up, went into the living room in my pajamas, and saw a filthy drunk man sleeping and snoring on our living room couch. The man was somebody Dad brought home from a bar. Dad had a soft spot in his heart for 'those that were down on their luck.'

* * *

In the summer of 1976, we moved twenty miles away from Wheelersburg to Minford, Ohio. Mom said that anytime they would accumulate equity in the house and Dad figured it out, he would sell the house and spend all the money.

Wheelersburg had a population of about 6,000. Minford's population was around 600 in the town. Rural Minford sits in the rolling hills of the Appalachian Plateau and the unglaciated Allegheny Plateau. Locals nicknamed these Appalachian foothills near Shawnee State Park and Forest the "Little Smokies."

In hindsight the move was probably the best thing that could have happened to me during the few months when I lost myself, when my heart lost hope and I shifted gears into reverse. I didn't have the foresight to see past the immediate trauma and didn't have anyone to help guide me through it. I was afraid to ask for help.

Our new next-door neighbors in Minford opened their arms to us. They were the sweetest family and invited me to share in their Sunday breakfast ritual of "Shit on Shingles" topped off with a sixteen-ounce bottle of Pepsi. I obliged kindly. They made gravy from sausage grease and covered each piece of toast with big ladle of "Shit." The sausage gravy and toast were chased down with big gulps of Pepsi until the plates were clean and the bottles empty. I thought I had died and gone to hog heaven. They invited me back each Sunday for more "shit."

Dad started working again, only this time for a trucking company and not with his own broken-down truck, so our household felt pretty normal for the first time in a long time.

After moving to Minford, I got my driver's license. Granny let me borrow her Ford Futura to take the driving portion of the test because the only car we had available was an old truck with a gear shift on the column of the steering wheel and a slipping clutch. My parents sold the station wagon to pay the mortgage when we were living in Wheelersburg. I could drive a stick shift but was afraid the instructor would fail me if the decrepit truck broke down. I needed a driver's license to get out of the sticks to do anything because my only social activity was eating "Shit on Shingles."

***

Our next-door neighbor Vicki was on a women's recreational softball team in Portsmouth and asked me to join. I previously pitched for the Wheelersburg high school girls' team and they needed a pitcher, so she said. I rode with her to the games and practices because we only had that old truck to drive and it wasn't to be used for leisurely activities.

The softball team was not a teenage girls' team. The players comprised of mostly older women who looked like rough farmers. Vicki was five years older than me. When I arrived for practice, they didn't know what to do with me. I wanted to pitch but the previous pitcher all of a sudden decided she wanted to pitch instead of playing shortstop.

I played every position on the field and they finally settled on me being a 5'6" 105-pound catcher with knocking knobby knees. During the first game as the catcher, a gigantic sized batter drove the ball long into the outfield and the center fielder missed the catch. The batter looked like a linebacker. She came barreling around third base. I took my position at home plate by straddling the plate in hopes of catching the ball and tagging her out when she slid. She decided not to slide. Instead, she bulldozed me. I flew into the air, into the metal fence, and landed on my ass. I lost my breath when I hit the back stop and gasped for air. I didn't have to be the catcher again after that. They finally let me pitch.

These older rural Appalachian women nicknamed me Renée Richards and started calling me Renée. I didn't understand and was really confused about what they meant. I asked Mom about Renée Richards. I thought she must be a famous women's softball pitcher because I could throw a great high arched pitch and could hit any corner of the plate with accuracy. I thought it was a compliment.

I was terribly confused when Mom told me Renée Richards was transgender. I couldn't understand why these mean women called me her name. I was a good athlete but I was not a man nor did I look or act like one. Mom told me that there would be plenty of people in my life who would challenge me for being a strong and independent woman. She said that I would have to learn to rise above them and ignore their remarks. She said that I was smart and should not allow ignorant people to get in my way. She gave me the book *Great American Poets* by Emily Dickinson to make me feel better. Mom always provided encouragement and found things for me to read that would sooth my soul.

* * *

At Minford high school, if you showed up for the first basketball practice you were on the team. It's hard to field a team in a town with only six hundred people, but they were serious about their girls' sports. I was the starting point guard.

While changing from school clothes to practice shorts and a t-shirt at the first basketball practice, I noticed most of the girls on the team wore boy's underwear. When I asked why, they told me that boys' cotton underwear doesn't ride up your ass like the girl's silky underwear and suggested that I give it a try.

It was a sight to see several girls wearing a garment that suggested equipment was inside and ready to sprout out. All I could do was chuckle. I couldn't get myself to ask Mom to buy me boy's underwear, and I wasn't about to wear my brother's. I didn't want to have anything to do with this new athletic wardrobe advancement for girls. I asked for cowboy hats, bb guns, holsters, buster brown t-shirts, and Keds sneakers just like my brother's in the past, but this request could push Mom over the edge so it just didn't happen. I was the odd girl out in this case which was unusual for me.

We were just getting started with basketball when Mom and Dad said we were moving again. Dad took a job working as a long-haul driver for the trucking company Roadway Services in Toledo. Living in Minford was the shortest time we had spent in one place yet, except for the temporary trailer before we moved into our house on Filmore Lane in Wheelersburg. Wheelersburg ended up being the longest place that I lived while growing up, five years total.

13

Epiphany

Mom enrolled us at Bowsher high school in Toledo, Ohio at the beginning of basketball season. Bowsher was a AAA high school and Minford and Wheelersburg were single A schools. Girls actually had to try out to play on the team and some were not selected. I didn't know this when I went to my first basketball practice. Nobody told me that I was trying out. I thought that by showing up I was on the team.

After practice finished the coach handed me a uniform and game schedule. The other girls on the team wouldn't talk to me. I heard them whispering in the locker that it wasn't fair that I could just show up for practice and be on the team when their friends couldn't.

I went to each practice and gave it everything that I had. These girls were better than the boys that I played with in Wheelersburg. Our team won second in state during my junior year.

In Toledo girls' basketball started as a league sport in the 1969-70 school years. They didn't wait until Title IX forced them to have girls' sports teams or lose their government funding. Bowsher H.S.

even had a junior high school team to prepare young girls to become good athletes.

At practice our coach ran us up and down the court for a solid hour. We didn't stop running suicides, performing shooting and passing drills, and running line drills until we were ready to drop dead. Our practices in Toledo were ten times harder than my previous practice's in the rural schools.

The next hour we practiced playing games and learning offensive and defensive strategies. I learned how to work harder than I had ever worked in my young life. The intense level of discipline that I was taught from my basketball coach gave me a lifelong lesson and skill of not giving up and learning how to push myself past a place that I never thought that I was capable of going. Even when I felt like vomiting, I didn't quit. Basketball continued to be my saving grace, saving me from self-destruction. Basketball kept me shifting gears forward.

* * *

I signed up for the same classes that I was taking in Minford since we transferred schools in the middle of the semester. When I showed up in the Home Economics class I was completely surprised because this was not rural home economics where you learned how to can and sew your first apron (that I still have). They didn't have a 4-H Club either. And, suburb people buy their meat and produce from the super market instead raising their own cows or going to a local farm or butcher for meat.

When I walked into the class room the girl students were the ones considered as "burn outs" by the popular crowd. They were thought to be squeaking by and trying to get enough credits to graduate thinking Home Economics was an easy class.

That was not true in my new class. Yes, some of the girls appeared to be financially disadvantaged and were making plans to go to a trade school instead of college but they weren't a bunch of burnouts. We all loved the teacher. She was really happy to have me in class and made me feel welcome. With her guidance I was able to take my skills to a completely new level and not just learn how to make my clothes because we didn't have any money to buy store clothes.

I took this class seriously and learned how to make wonderful delicate pastries, puddings, cakes, and fabulous healthy meals. It wasn't just about cooking and canning. Our teacher was passionate about teaching her students broad information related to financial skills, furniture design styles, and textile concepts and principles, just to name a few. I even learned how to set a formal table and what utensils to use for meals with multiple courses. I loved learning about things that I could actually apply.

* * *

After basketball season was over, I took a job working at Ponderosa Steak House making minimum wage of $2.30 an hour. In tax year 1977, I made $2,284. That's 931 hours of part time work busing tables, pouring drinks, and filling up salad bar containers.

In today's dollars, that equates to $9,500 – a lot of money for a 16-17-year-old teenager.

At Ponderosa, I began as a person who cleaned off tables after people left the restaurant and was called a "busser." "Bussers" carried large gray plastic bins from vacated table to table stacking heavy white ceramic plates and gold plastic drink glasses into the bin while scraping left over food to the side to make it easier for the dish washer to load into the massive washing machine.

Ponderosa had an interesting business concept. Customers entered a line to order food and drinks and pay ahead of time. A server delivered the food to the table. A food server worked for 50% of minimum wage, or $1.15 per hour because they occasionally received tips. Only at Ponderosa Steak House, customers didn't know to leave a tip because they had to stand in line to order food and get drinks. That concept just didn't work well for the servers. It was difficult for the restaurant to keep them employed. As soon as they got a little experience they left for a real server's job.

After school I worked a four-hour shift throughout weekdays and an eight hour shift each Saturday and Sunday. Dinner was free and I started putting on weight from eating the delicious buttery buns and cheese cake. From anywhere in the steakhouse I could smell when the rolls were baked to perfection. We didn't burn any rolls on my shift. The entire crew worked hard as a team and we created tons of fun along the way.

The weekend janitor quit so the general manager asked me if I wanted to become the janitor. I proudly took the job. I was also happy to wear jeans instead of the itchy crotch snap red checkered polyester body suit. Even after washing the used body suit in hot water it still smelled like grease from the grill.

As a weekend janitor I clocked in at 6 a.m. to accept truck deliveries and rotate the meat and stock. A large disgusting guy that delivered the towels early Saturday mornings came inside and went into the bathroom for an hour with a magazine. After the second week of polluting the entire restaurant for hours from his weeklong sewage backup release, I created a new towel policy that under strict orders no towel vendors were allowed inside the building until the manager showed up at 9 a.m. I had enough of his shit.

I started bulking up with arm and leg muscles from the janitor job of lifting chairs and mopping. Each wooden chair weighed about 35 pounds. There were two hundred and fifty of them. I had to stack them on top of the tables before mopping.

First, I got into squatting position, placed one hand on the bottom leg of the chair while holding onto the top, raised up and flipped the chair upside down as I returned from the squat position. As the chair flew through the air, I placed it cushion side down on top of the table and repeated the process two hundred and fifty times.

After mopping the entire restaurant with a long commercial grade mop by swirling it from side to side and wringing it out in a big yellow bucket, I flipped each chair back to the six-inch red square tile floor. That paid workout added up to one thousand squats and curls each weekend.

One morning I watered the English Ivy in the hanging plants surrounding the top of the salad bar. I noticed marijuana plants sprouting from the dirt of the English Ivy. The contrast of the dark green ivy and the bright green sprouts stood out like a sore thumb. When the other workers came in, we all got a big laugh out of the discovered treasure.

The general manager didn't find it as funny as we did. He said that we could be shut down for growing pot in the store. The plants thrived from the steaming water filled pan under the hot food portion

Left-Right-Left

of the salad bar. The continuous illuminated florescent lights above the plants helped them sprout. For the next half hour, I dug through the planters, weeded out each baby pot plant, and handed the tiny leaves over to the general manager for proper disposal, somewhere.

When the weekend grill cook snuck out early, before cleaning the thick steak grease off the wall behind the grill, I got stuck with doing it in the morning. I had to spray the wall with some horrible chemical and let it soak into the hardened grease. Then I used a putty knife to scrape the grease from wall while inhaling the toxic fumes from the aerosol can of degreaser. I treated myself to an extra piece of cheese cake for the effort.

Another job was flipping ribeye steak packages over while they thawed on large trays in the cooler after being taken out of the freezer the night before. The ribeye's were shot full of purple tenderizer when they were packaged at the factory. As the ribeye's thawed in the plastic casings, the tenderizer soaked into the meat so they would fall apart in your mouth when you chewed them. People would say, "Those ribeye's are so tender!"

After seeing the purple chemical swirling in the red blood from the meat thawing overnight, I quit eating ribeye steaks. The little purple pucks just weren't appealing anymore. I stuck with the New York strip steaks that weren't chemically treated.

Initially I didn't think a thing about the half gallon scoop of white powder that was dumped into the large white plastic garbage bin used to store dozens of heads of lettuce that were chopped up each morning and placed into a bin by the Asian prep lady who spoke little English.

In her very broken English she said that she married a military man and came to the United States. She was not happy. The prep lady took each head of lettuce with her two hands and hit the core of the head on the table with a striking force then plucked the core right out of the head. Then she held a big chopping knife in her hand, raised her arm like granny use to do to cut off the chicken's head at the tree stump and struck the knife twice on the cutting board. Two quick hits quartered the head before she tossed the lettuce into the bin. She was fast. The bin filled up quickly.

When the bin was full of lettuce, she took the garden hose and filled the bin with water until the lettuce quarters were floating. Next, she took a plastic scoop big enough to hold two sacks of flour and reached into another large plastic outdoor garbage size bin, scooped out the white chemical powder and dumped it into the lettuce bin. Lastly, she reached into the bin with her tiny arms and dissolved the white power into the lettuce by rotating her arms like an electric mixer. I asked her, "Why are you putting powder in the lettuce?" She said in her Asian accent, "No brown lettuce." I stopped eating lettuce on the salad bar.

Dennis Jr. worked at McDonalds across the street from Ponderosa Steak House. He also worked the evening shifts and picked me up from my evening shift after work so I wouldn't have to walk five miles home in the dark and cross a major four lane highway. All minors were required by law to get off at certain times depending on whether school was in session or not so we always had the same schedule.

One evening Dennis Jr. wasn't there to pick me up after work ended. I used the office phone to call home and nobody answered. It was late. I was tired and needed to study before going to bed. I waited for Dennis Jr. a half hour before making the decision to walk five miles home down Secor to Byrne Road.

As I walked alongside the dark four-lane busy road, a nice-looking man in his thirties stopped his car and asked me if I would like to have a ride. I said, "No thank you" and continued to walk. He said that it was really cold and that I could freeze to death out there. I thought about it and figured it would be a lot faster to get home if I took the ride so I got in the car. I didn't think a thing about it or that it could be dangerous.

It was 1977 and common for people to hitch-hike and catch rides. He asked me where I was going and I instructed him how to get to my house. He said, "Are you sure you want to go home?" I said, "Of course I want to go home. I need to do homework and get to bed before school in the morning." He asked me how old I was and I said, "Sixteen." It was only a month before my seventeenth birthday. After his questioning began, I got really nervous and scared. I knew something was terribly wrong and that I wasn't going home, not then and maybe not ever. When he stopped at a stop sign, I jumped out of the car and ran for my life though back yards of homes until I found a place to hide and waited until it felt safe to leave. I cut through neighborhoods until I finally got home. I didn't tell Mom and Dad that I got into a stranger's car for fear of getting into trouble. I told Dennis Jr. and he was never late picking me up from work again.

***

In year 1978 Toledo was hit with a blizzard that produced 30-40 inches of snow with up to twenty feet of reported snow drifts. For days we couldn't get the car out of the driveway. People used snow mobiles to help others get needed supplies.

We rarely saw Dad. According to him, he worked twenty-four hours a day and was only home one day a week. Even during the blizzard of 1978, he drove the semi-truck for Roadway.

Dad was making enough money and could afford to buy me a used car. I didn't realize that you had to slow the car down when crossing a railroad track. I thought it was fun speeding over the tracks on my way to school and getting a little air under the wheels.

The Fastback Volkswagen heater barely blew out cold air in the bitter cold temperatures. I had to stick my head out the driver's side window to see to drive. As soon as I scraped the ice off the windows, they would freeze right back up from the steam of my breath. The cold air from the window and the sweat from basketball practice froze my hair stiff like icicles too.

Over a few weeks the steering wheel of my little car began to vibrate, a little at a time. Then it started shaking violently. Finally, one day while driving to school I heard a loud snap and the car went off to the side of the road by itself. Dad said the tie rod broke and it would cost more to fix it then the car was worth.

Dad and Dennis Jr. pulled the car home with a rope. It sat in front of the house until Dad sold it for two hundred dollars, the amount he paid for it.

By this time Dennis Jr. had acquired a Chevy van and a souped up 1970 Dodge Charger. He let me drive the Charger to school and work. He drove the Chevy. I guess he felt guilty for not picking me up from work the night that I almost didn't come home again, at least not the same way I left that day. It shouldn't have been his responsibility, but he looked after me after that incident.

He taught me how to drive the Charger. There was a huge difference from driving the little Volkswagen that barely got up to thirty-five miles an hour. When I squeaked out the clutch on the Charger the tires would spin and it took off like a bat out of hell. It seemed to start off at thirty-five miles an hour. It scared me to death to drive the hot rod but Dennis Jr. just laughed and was proud of me for handling the car. He never complained about me driving it.

* * *

I came home from work one day and Dad had beaten Mom almost to death. He blamed her for everything that was wrong in his mind, that he had to work too much, that he was never home, that the driving schedule was too strict, that the weather was too harsh to drive a truck, and on and on and on.

Roadway didn't allow Mom to go with him to work. It appeared that this beating was the last straw for her. We quickly gathered a few clothes in a suitcase and loaded them in Dennis Jr.'s van and headed south on Hillbilly Highway to Greenup. We were going "home" again.

We got as far as Columbus, Ohio before it started snowing hard. Dennis Jr. could hardly keep the van from sliding all over the road. A car behind us couldn't stop and slid into the back of the van. Luckily nobody got hurt, but we weren't off to a good start.

After a week in Greenup Dad came down to bring his family back once again, only this time he invented a new plan. He decided that we were going to move to sunny Florida where snow and harsh wintery weather didn't exist.

I wasn't happy with this announcement. I didn't want to go to a fourth high school. I checked with the school counselor about options. She said that I had enough credits and all the necessary classes to graduate from high school at the end of my junior year and so did

Left-Right-Left

Dennis Jr. I had taken all college preparatory classes during high school.

My original plan had been to take it easier my senior year. Not that I would have done that by the time senior year rolled around. Granny would say that if you let grass grow under your feet, it'll start growing on of the top of your coffin.

* * *

In the spring after the snow melted in Toledo, our family took a "vacation" to Florida. It was really an exploration of the state to find a place to live. We drove down I75 and stopped at a couple tourist traps like Homosassa Springs and rode in the glass bottom boats to see fish swimming around in the crystal blue river.

Mostly we just rode in the car for days and slept in flea bag hotels, literally. One night I had so many flea bites on my body that I went into the parking lot and slept in the car that I had just been in for fifteen hours.

We didn't have any reservations for a place to sleep. We just looked for "Vacancy" on the neon sign glowing in the front of the motel and kept driving until we found the cheapest motel with a room available.

Mom asked for a "hideaway" bed for me to sleep in and my brothers shared the other double bed in the tiny rooms. A maid would roll my bed down the parking lot and dropped it off in front of our room. The only motels we stayed in had outside entrances.

I didn't know what a hotel with elevators was because we didn't stay in those fancy places. My brothers and I wanted to stay in a place with a pool. Not that we had time to swim in it.

After scouring a portion of the east coast on A1A and discovering that it was too expensive to live near the water, we headed west and landed in the Tampa Bay area. Mom's brother lived in Tampa. Dad decided that we would live there. We rarely saw our uncle but my parents wanted to be close to family. Having family nearby made it seem like we wouldn't be all alone in Florida like we were in Toledo.

* * *

Back in Ohio, I passed an Armed Services recruiting station on my way home from work and had an epiphany about joining the military. I had noticed recruiting signs at school, but didn't pay any attention to them because I assumed that I would go to college in Ohio. I thought I could possibly get a basketball scholarship to pay for tuition.

When I returned to school, I walked into the basketball coach's office and sadly told him that I wouldn't be playing on the team next year. He understood all the reasons, wished me well, and was really sorry that I couldn't play on the team. He told me that I had a bright future ahead of me and not to let anything stand in my way.

I went to the military recruiting office and spoke with all the different branch representatives. I didn't want to join the Navy because I get motion sick. I thought the Air Force would be a better fit. I took the Armed Services Vocational Aptitude Battery test used to determine which occupations I could qualify for enlistment in the United States Armed Forces. My scores were high.

The recruiter thought that I would be a really good Aerospace Warning and Control Systems Operator. I didn't know what that was, but he said it was like an enlisted version of being an Air Traffic Controller. I had a cousin by marriage that was an Air Traffic Controller and made a ton of money. It sounded good to me.

Since I was only seventeen years old my parents had to sign for me to enter the military under the delayed enlistment program. The Air Force didn't have an opening for this position for months. The United States was not in wartime in 1977, so I had to get on a list to get in or take a job that I didn't want to do. I didn't want to be in the infantry or a cook, where plenty of jobs were available. I decided to wait.

Dennis Jr. and I graduated from Bowsher high school a year early for me and on schedule for him. As soon as we graduated Mom and

Dad sold the house. We packed the U-Haul and headed to Brandon, Florida, a suburb of Tampa.

In the spring of 1978 in Brandon I found a job working at a door factory on the assembly line in an extremely loud environment while I waited to enter the military. As each exterior aluminum door approached me on the conveyor belt, I took a long strip of aluminum and beat it into the side of the door with a rubber coated steel sledge hammer for eight hours a day, five days a week.

Every second I pounded that sledge hammer and listened to everyone's sledge hammers striking blows. I vowed to get my college education so I didn't have to work on assembly lines whacking steel like granny had to do to earn money to raise her five kids.

The shifts were eight-hours long, plus a half hour to eat a bagged lunch of a bologna sandwich and chips that didn't require refrigeration because it was so full of preservatives. At the end of each shift, everyone literally ran to the one- and only-time card machine at the end of the building. People pushed others, grabbed the paper card that displayed their scribbled name, inserted the card into the metal clock, listened for the time stamp, and ran as fast as they could out the door.

Once in the car it was like riding the bumper cars at the carnival. People backed into other cars and hit each other in the parking lots while shooting lots of middle fingers in the air. Each worker tried to be the first one to get to the local bar two blocks down the road to get a good seat, have a few beers, and complain about the job that they just left and hated.

Nobody cared about their cars. The more bangs the higher the social status. It meant that they were faster than anyone else getting out of aluminum door prison so they could laugh at everyone else who entered next. It was a game of releasing frustration for some. Dents were highly valued. I lasted a month before resigning and entering into my next phase as an Airman in the United States Air Force.

14

Military

Dennis Jr. and Danny were so proud of me for joining the Air Force. Dennis wanted to join too but had flat feet so they military wouldn't enlist him. I left on a Grey Hound bus to Jacksonville, Florida to begin processing before entering basic training a couple weeks later.

At the time, we were living in a small run-down trailer while Mom and Dad looked for a house to purchase. Again, owning a house was Mom's American's Dream, but she never owned any of the houses they purchased; the bank did, with a thirty-year mortgage each time they moved. As soon as equity built up in the house, Dad had to sell, spend the money, and move to greener pastures.

Dad got a job hauling watermelons from Florida to the North Eastern states using someone else's semi-truck and trailer. Mom remained unemployed. Money was tight. I assumed the Air Force would provide everything I needed so I gave Mom and Dad the rest of my aluminum door pounding money before I left.

I had two-hundred dollars in my pocket when I flew to San Antonio for basic training. Mom said that I wanted to change the world. At the time I just wanted to have a stable life with some semblance of starting a career.

I was told by several older veterans before I left home not to volunteer for anything. I tried to keep a low profile and check things out for the first few days in basic training. When one of the originally appointed squad leaders didn't fulfill her obligations, the drill sergeant appointed me as the replacement. I signed an official letter accepting the additional responsibility. I wasn't worried. I wanted to be a leader. The military was going to give me a chance. I was ready to take on that responsibility.

There were fifty women in our squadron. A typical day looked like this:

0445: Reveille.

0500-0600: Exercise.

0600-0615: Breakfast.

0630-0745: Clean dorm

0800-1130: Class and drills.

1130-1230: Lunch.

1300-1700: Class and drills.

1700-1800: Dinner.

1900: Clean dorm.

2100: Lights out when you hear "Taps."

Each squad leader was responsible for twelve or thirteen airmen. My bed was at the head of all the other women under my leadership. When the drill sergeant wasn't around, I was responsible for the airman's actions and behavior. If they did something wrong the drill sergeant yelled at me, not them.

The drill sergeant would get an inch from my face and start berating me as the other women stood at attention and watched. Some of them were scared to death. I knew it was a game and didn't take it personally. I was already accustomed to hard discipline and team work from my basketball coach in Toledo. I wasn't afraid of the yelling. I had grown mentally and physically stronger than when in my fearful and timid childhood. I stood tall, only this time I didn't protest. I took the yelling in stride, just like Dennis Jr. used to do. I learned from him to be strong.

It was my job to teach and train the others in my squad how to be perfect in an imperfect world. The military expected perfection and didn't stop until they got it. This effort taught us discipline and perseverance. It wasn't easy, but necessary to work as a team and not as individuals. You traded in your individuality when you signed up to give your life for your country. It wasn't about what your country could do for you.

During one of many dorm inspections all the women stood at attention in front of their beds. The drill sergeant walked down the line stopping in front of each airman's bed checking to make sure their shoes were spit shined, underwear and socks stacked perfectly in the drawer, clothes spaced in the closet two inches between each hanger and on and on with rules teaching discipline.

There was usually an episode of embarrassment during each inspection to teach humility. The humiliating episodes became less and less common as we became better at embracing military standards.

Half way down the line the drill sergeant found a "fuzz bunny" next to an airman's dress shoe under the bed. This gave him an opportunity to go berserk and play another game. A "fuzz bunny" was just a small wad of dust like cat hair that flies around. Dust of any kind during inspection warranted a big fat violation. He picked up the "fuzz bunny" and placed it at the front of the line on the floor next to my bed.

He briefly yelled at me then told the unlucky airman whose shoe put a stop to the "fuzz bunny" to march to the front of the line. Then he instructed her to get on her hands and knees and blow the "fuzz bunny" to the end of the line as each of the other airman watched her crawl past them. She tried to keep the small dust ball in a straight line without it getting trapped under the bed or into someone else's shoes.

These embarrassing Moments seemed to motivate the troops to work harder so they didn't have to craw on their hands and knees like a dog and blow dust around on a thickly waxed shinny floor in front of their peers while getting ridiculed by the drill sergeant. Sometimes that alone made my teaching job easier. I motivated my team by being more of a nurturer and teacher when some women cried after failing attempts to do things right. I had to wait until the drill sergeant left to provide encouragement and support.

When the drill sergeant found out that I ran track in high school I was charged with leading the fifty troops in our squadron around the track for our daily one-and-a-half-mile run. It was a challenging job because I couldn't see what was behind me or on my side. I had to keep my head straight while running in the front of the squadron. I learned to tell if I was going too fast by listening for the cadence of the troops' steps that were behind me. If someone was out of step, I could hear them and I would slow down until everyone was back in step.

To get our minds off the misery of running in the hot and humid heat of Texas in the summer, we sang tunes to stay in step like, "Left, left, left-right-left. My back aches I'm all uptight my hips shake from left to right, left, left, left-right-left." The songs helped us stay in step as a team. The cadence kept us moving forward and not focusing on the pain. I've kept this cadence in my head my entire life – move forward and work through the pain…left, left, left-right-left, one step at a time.

Our squadron was only as good as the weakest person. I kept a pace that ensured everyone could run in step and in formation at the same time. The pace increased daily so we could finish on time together on the last day where it counted most. If you didn't run faster than the maximum allocated time on the final run you got "washed out" meaning given a second chance to go through basic training again.

I can't imagine that anyone would ever want to do that again. We were committed to not leave anyone behind. In the military you work, live, play, and thrive together. If one person didn't pull their weight then the rest of the team tried to help them get up to speed. These lessons stayed with me through my life in corporate America. Years later, I had to laugh after I told one of my corporate teammates that there was no "I" in TEAM when he said there was a "ME." He moved on to a new company and wasn't missed.

It was hot as hell in San Antonio, Texas at the end of July when we had our timed run on race day. When we reached the finish line, we weren't all in step, but we held hands with those who struggled to make sure they made it across the line on time. Nobody got left behind in our squadron.

I wrote home every week while I was in basic training and continued writing when I got stationed in Berlin, Germany. Recently, I found out that Mom kept all my letters. Here's an excerpt from a letter dated May 27, 1978, written while I was in basic training: "A girl left her security drawer open and got $40 (two twenties) stolen. Everyone is in an uproar here. We want to give the girl a dollar from each of us but don't want to pay for her mistake because she should have known better than to leave the drawer open. We all learned a lesson to keep our security drawer locked. We aren't telling our training instructor because it would get everyone in trouble and we sure don't need him on the warpath any more than he already is. The girl is very upset. We are going to give the person who stole the money a chance to turn it in by after church tomorrow secretly. If the money isn't turned in then we will lend Phyllis a dollar a piece. She can pay us back whenever she can."

Situations like these provided valuable lessons for us. We had to figure out how to live and work together. As young adults we were starting to learn how to think independently but act as a team to figure out problems logically and fairly. We learned how to find the best solutions to life's dilemmas within a safe environment.

It was also a time to educate myself about people who were different from me. When I joined the military, women in my squadron were of many races. We showered in a large empty room with several shower heads close together on each of the four sterile walls. I stood in line with a wrapped towel until it was my turn to drop it. My knees knocked from fright.

I had rarely seen a naked person. Now I was witnessing a room full of naked women of all colors. I tried to look away but it was like seeing a car accident and rubber necking on the highway.

When it was my turn to shower, I was afraid to take off the towel. In our school gym class, we showered individually behind a curtain. Now, I was exposing what felt like my soul to the world. I wasn't prepared for baring my assets.

I hadn't seen my own body naked. We didn't have a full-length mirror growing up, not that I would have stared into it. We were modest. My brothers weren't allowed to run around in their underwear and neither was I. For whatever reason seeing someone in a bathing suit was different, accepting.

The unveiling was the beginning of pealing back a lifetime of ignorant remarks that I heard in my childhood. But even as a young child, I did not see people of color different than me. But I heard comments that were degrading to people of any color and women in general. The comments were always from men, never from women.

* * *

While in basic training, I met a guy who seemed really nice and strikingly handsome. I saw him occasionally on base. We briefly exchanged words because he spoke little English, but his face shined with happiness. Our military trained Saudi Arabia officers.

At the end of basic training we were granted a pass for a day off during the eight and a half weeks of training. It was a big deal to go shopping in downtown San Antonio, Texas for the day. A military bus dropped us off downtown and we had to be back at the dorm by 7:30 pm.

My Saudi friend and I agreed to explore downtown together. He met me at the bus drop off point. He said that he knew where it was located. That should have been my first clue. Apparently, he had been there before.

When I got off the bus, he suggested that we go to his apartment for a glass of water before shopping and walking around. It was blazing hot in the middle of July. He said his apartment was only two blocks away. I didn't see any harm in his offer, but a little voice told me otherwise. I was on guard entering into his apartment and checked around for exit doors.

In full dress uniform, I sat nervously on the couch as he brought me a class of water. He said that he had to use the restroom and would be out in a minute. After ten minutes I started fidgeting, got up and starting pacing. I wasn't used to sitting around for any period of time.

To my surprise, he came out of the bathroom without a stitch of clothes on. It was the second time that I had seen a fully naked man. The first one stepped onto the front porch stoop while I walked home from school in second grade. Only this time the naked man was ten feet away from me with a penis that looked a mile-long dangling from his slender body. I screamed from shock and ran to the exit door as fast as I could get out of there in my military dress uniform and heels. I ran to the bus stop, then toward the shopping area to find other women in uniform. I told many women airman about my experience with the Saudi man. I wonder how many others didn't get a chance to escape.

I don't remember the exact date, apartment, where the bus dropped us off, the rest of the day or even what the man was wearing before he vanished into the bathroom. I will never forget the slender muscular naked body of the man who deceived me and was coming after me before I turned to run out the door. It never occurred to me that we were going to his apartment to have sex or that I could possibly be raped. I had just turned eighteen the month before entering basic training and never even had a boyfriend before that time.

* * *

My first assignment after basic training and technical school was at McCord Air Force Base near Tacoma, Washington. I made $4,200 my first year in the military. I earned $132 every two weeks. When I got to technical school after basic training, I bought a pair of polyester military dress pants for an outrageously high price of $21.75 so I could limit the times I needed to wear the skirt and hot suffocating pantyhose. I worked almost two days to buy one pair of uniform pants. Skirts were issued but not pants. I also bought combat boots because they weren't issued to women either, only men. I purchased a radio with an eight-track player and a new blouse. That took care of my two weeks of pay.

With my next check I bought a Kodak Vivitar 600 film camera with a built-in flash for $35. I wanted to get a Yashica FR-II for $200 but decided that purchase would need to wait for a long time. The FR-II was an auto-exposure Single-Lens Reflex (SLR) camera. I loved taking pictures and the Vivitar camera was the beginning of a lifelong passion of photography for me. I vowed to get the better camera as soon as I could afford it. I was trying to learn how to manage money on my own.

First, I needed a car. It was difficult to get to work from my dorm on the sprawling base because I had to walk to work and everywhere else. Trying to buy my first car proved to be a big challenge. I didn't have any credit and I couldn't establish credit without having credit.

I had to save up $300 and give it to the base credit union to hold before they would issue me a credit card with a $300 limit. I could borrow against my own money at a twelve percent interest rate. But if I was a man, I could obtain a credit card with no problem and no upfront cash. The rumor at the time was the credit union thought women would get pregnant, leave the military (not by choice) and default on their loans.

After three month of no late payments they would raise my credit limit to $500 but still hold onto my $300. If I wanted to buy a car, I first had to establish that I wasn't a bad credit risk and would be reevaluated after six months. That's the way it was in 1978.

Purchasing a car required a down payment of twenty-five percent. The interest on the loan was twelve percent. After several months of walking miles to work, the chow hall, the gym, and my dorm in the cold winter rain at McCord AFB, I finally saved up enough money to purchase a maroon 1970 Opel Manta with seventy thousand miles on it for one thousand dollars cash. It took every dime I had. Insurance was $19 a month. I felt good about not having a car payment hanging over my head. Getting something on credit seemed like a really bad idea.

* * *

Tacoma, Washington was a beautiful place to live. I learned how to ski at Mt. Rainer. I appreciated the intense beauty of the forests and the majestic sky. I loved the surrounding area. But, I didn't particularly like working shift work as an Aerospace Warning and Control Systems Operator (AC&W). My shift consisted of working two-days, then two swing or afternoons, then two midnights and finally three days off. My first "day off" started the morning I got off the midnight shift.

We were nicknamed "Scope Dopes." My job was sort of like a civilian Air Traffic Controller, but I only watched the aircraft on the radar scope. I didn't control aircraft like the recruiter suggested. Only officers controlled the military aircraft and fighter jets.

Aerospace Control and Warning encompasses the functions involved in aerospace surveillance and aerospace vehicle detection, including missile warning systems, controlling, and plotting the movement of aircraft displayed on a radar scope.

AC&W Operators manage and operate systems that include functions involving electronic warfare, surveillance, data link management, identification and weapons control. We provided radar control and monitoring of air weapons during both offensive and defensive air operations. We also provided surveillance and identification of any aircraft that came within U.S. airspace.

I learned an immense amount of information in this position and how to analyze problems and potential threats. Working together as a team was critical to the mission of keeping our skies safe against attacks from foreign powers. This high stress analytical job prepared me for a future of analyzing data and solving problems in my civilian career.

I met my first girlfriend at McCord Air Force Base. Sherri was a First Lieutenant right out of Officer's Training School (OTS). We arrived at McCord near the same time. I was walking past the softball field when I first saw her fielding a ground ball. As a shortstop, she scooped the ball into her glove and side-armed it like a bullet to the first baseman with confidence. Her athletic skills were soon acquired by the U.S. Armed Services Women's team.

In the military, being chosen to play for a Department of Defense (D.O.D.) team was like being selected for the Olympics. Basically, you got to play sports during parts of the year as your full-time paid job. The Air Force, Army, Navy, and Marines each had a softball team where players were recruited each year to play in a national tournament.

Mary was eight years older and two inches shorter than me with dark cropped hair and green eyes. She was a competitive swimmer in college and an all-around athlete that could play any sport. I was instantly attracted to her swag (At one time SWAG stood for 'Secretly We Are Gay'). She stood out in the field like it was hers and the rest of the team followed her commands.

I sat on the bleachers and watched the team practice. I knew I could pitch better than the woman on the mound but my household goods hadn't arrived at the base yet, so I didn't have a glove to play with. I left without being noticed. I came back the next week with my glove and asked if I could practice with the team.

The coach tried me out in every position except pitching when I told him that I wanted to pitch. I couldn't catch a fly in the outfield to save my life. I couldn't play infield because I was afraid the ball would hit me in the face. The only position I knew and loved was pitching. If the ball came at me off the bat, I instantly reacted and caught it. I didn't miss. I had quick reflexes. If I had too much time to think about catching a ball from a hit off the bat I would mess up and it would hit me in the face. The effect wasn't any different for me than playing tennis. I love to play at the net but the base line gives me way too much time to screw up a shot.

Finally, when the coach found that I was useless for anything else he let me pitch. I threw the ball with a really high arch, before height restrictions were imposed in slow pitch softball. I could place it at any corner of the plate with each pitch. I had years of practice pitching softballs into a bucket at home. The pitch gracefully rolled off the end of my fingertips after a deep squat and that got Sherri's attention. That arch was a rainbow of happiness for me but only for a short while. Sherri liked young airman.

When she went off to play on the D.O.D. team for that annual tournament, she found a new recruit to play with. I would have never known about the affair if it hadn't been for a woman that I went to technical school with who was also on the D.O.D. team. When she told me about the closeness of the two players, I didn't want to believe it. I asked Sherri about what I heard and she lied to me. I could tell right away. That was the end of that.

It was tough being gay in the military and difficult to confide in anyone about personal issues. To make matters worse, co-workers and bosses would ask or say,

"Do you have a boyfriend?"

"Why not?"

"There are plenty of guys to choose from on the base."

"Do you want to have kids?"

"Why not?"

"You mean you didn't come in the military to find a husband?"

The conversations were always awkward and essentially resulted in not having close personal relationships with any of my co-workers because I feared disclosure would get me disgracefully kicked out of the military. For those like me, we were seen by co-workers as all business because we had to hide who we were inside. We couldn't trust anyone with our deep secret of being gay.

On my next assignment in the early 1980's when I was stationed at Homestead Air Force Base in Florida, I was continuously sexually harassed by my boss. Every time I walked by him, he would tell me how good my ass looked in my high dollar uniform pants. I was working out at the gym on my lunch hour every day. He complimented my muscular body on a regular basis. I shrugged it off and ignored him.

I was worried that if I said something to him it would bring attention to me resulting in an investigation that could inadvertently determine my sexuality. If discovered that I was gay, I would be persecuted and kicked out of the military with a dishonorable discharge.

My gay friends joined the military swearing an oath in front of God that they weren't homosexual. If suspected that you were gay, the military would investigate by putting decoys on the softball team to collect any information they could conjure up. Then, they would interrogate and prosecute each person, one at a time, by kicking them to the street with a dishonorable discharge. They would coerce each gay person to give up the identity of another gay person that they knew or heard of being gay. Many service men and women became homeless after being kicked out.

During this time, I had a straight friend who was being investigated for being gay because she played on the military base softball team. During this investigation, my friend got married to a military man and her investigation ceased. Others weren't as lucky.

During the time my friend was under investigation, my boss came into my office and told me that I was summoned to see the base commander. Airmen First Class did not go see the base commander unless there was trouble. Immediately I thought that I had been discovered. I was scared to death.

My boss drove me to the base commander's office and didn't say a word and neither did I. I just knew my career was over and I felt sick. Where would I go? I couldn't go back to the abusive household and live with my parents again. I would become homeless within hours. My life would be disgraced and over. I thought that I would rather die than be dishonored and disgraced in front of the very country that I loved so much and was willing to give my life for.

I stood outside the commander's door with my boss standing at attention waiting for what seems like hours and hours when it was only a few minutes. When the commander summoned us inside, I stood in front of his desk and saluted. My knees were shaking. He said, "Airman Darnell, do you know why you are here?" I said, "No Sir." He said, "Have you done anything that would cause you to be here today?" I said, "Not to my knowledge, Sir." He smiled and said, "Airman Darnell, you have been promoted ahead of your peers." I gasped. If my knees had not been frozen straight because I was standing at attention, I would have collapsed. Now, I can live again.

I thought for sure I was getting the boot and would be a disgrace to myself and my country. Thank God I didn't confess after his frightful stern question when he stared me in the eyes trying to scare the shit out of me, and he did. I was powerless. He had all the power.

My boss had recommended me for early promotion. Only two airmen on the entire base got an early promotion that year, to my knowledge, and one was me. I was and still am beyond grateful.

Soon my boss began to tell me stories about his wife. He asked her to masturbate while he was having intercourse with her but she didn't want to touch herself. He asked me how I felt about this. I didn't have an answer. I was afraid to say anything.

I was working late at my desk and suddenly from behind someone reached their arms around my back and grabbed my breasts tightly and tried to fondle them. I jumped up from my chair terrified. I saw my boss' face and he looked surprised. I told him to never touch me again, and he didn't.

My work environment became uncomfortable and often hostile. I was constantly looking over my shoulder and nervous about being attacked again. I didn't work late again when nobody else was around. Within a couple of months, I got orders to go to Berlin and left the perpetrator behind.

During the early 1980's in the military classes on sexual harassment were not existent. I didn't have an avenue to tell anyone about an assault, especially if it was your boss assaulting you. We were never, not once taught how to handle situations of physical or sexual assault. Whatever came your way, you were expected to "man-up" and deal with it by yourself.

15

Commies

After Homestead AFB, I was stationed at Tempelhof Air Base in Berlin, Germany during the Cold War as an AC&W Operator. The Cold War began after World War II. The main players were the United States and the Soviet Union. The Cold War got its name because both sides were afraid of fighting each other directly so they fought indirectly. Hot Wars produce nuclear weapons. Cold Wars use words as weapons.

Tempelhof Central Airport (TCA) was a United States Military airfield in West Berlin, Germany between 1945 and 1994. Germany didn't use Tempelhof as a military airfield during World War II except for occasional emergency landings by fighter aircraft. The airfield was seized by the Soviet Union Red Army in April, 1945 and turned over to the United States in July the same year.

Earning the Air Force Commendation Medal at Tempelhof Air Base blessed me with being offered a tour of the city of Berlin with an army helicopter pilot. When I saw Tempelhof from above, the buildings were shaped like an eagle with its wings spread out. From the ground it didn't appear that all the buildings were attached, but I knew they were connected underground by a massive network of corridors. I took these pictures from the helicopter.

I purchased a Canon AE1 Program film camera from the Base Exchange and one by one lots of different lens to go with it. I took pictures everywhere I went while stationed in Berlin. I didn't have a dark room like Dad did for developing the images. I shot the images using rolls of Kodachrome slide film. I sent the rolls to New York City in a white and yellow envelop with a check for the cost of the returned slides. It took two to three weeks to get the slides back. I viewed the images in a handheld slide viewer. After a year, I purchased a slide projector and displayed the images on my white dorm room wall to share with my friends.

In June 1948, Soviet-led forces blocked all roads and railways leading to the western part of Berlin. President Truman quickly ordered military airplanes to fly coal, food, and medicine to the city. The planes kept coming, sometimes landing every few minutes, for more than a year. The United States received help from Britain and

France. Together they provided almost two and one-half million tons of supplies during two hundred-eighty thousand C-47 aircraft flights.

My job as an AC&W Operator was to protect the airspace surrounding the three air corridors that non-communist countries used to enter West Berlin through the communist East.

By 1961, tens of thousands of East Germans fled to the free West. East Germany's government decided to stop them by building a wall separating the eastern and western parts of the city of Berlin. Guards shot at anyone who tried to flee to the East by climbing over the wall.

Left-Right-Left

Some progress was made in easing Cold War tensions when Kennedy was president. In 1963, the two sides reached a major arms control agreement. They agreed to ban tests of nuclear weapons above ground, under water, and in space. They also established a direct telephone link between the White House and the Kremlin.

Checkpoint Charlie was constructed in 1961 when the communist East Germany Berlin Wall was erected. I took the top picture of Checkpoint Charlie (on the previous page) in 1985 and the bottom one in 2018. There were only three checkpoints for people from West Berlin to get out of the city. The other two were Checkpoint Alpha and Bravo. Charlie was located on Friedrichstrasse, a historic street in the American-occupied city center. Charlie was the only gateway where East Germany allowed Allied diplomats, military personnel, and foreign tourists to pass into Berlin's Soviet sector.

The United States, France, and Britain stationed military police at Checkpoint Charlie to ensure their officials had ready access to the border. The Allied guards spent most of their time monitoring diplomatic and military traffic, but they were also on hand to register and provide information to travelers before they ventured beyond the Wall.

In response to mass protests and international criticism, the East German government finally eased its travel restrictions in November 1989. The new policy was supposed to take effect in an orderly fashion, but it turned into a free-for-all after a government official misspoke during a press conference and said the law was changing right away.

That night, impromptu street parties broke out around Berlin. Thousands of East Germans gathered outside Checkpoint Charlie and other crossing points and began screaming for the guards to open the gates. Westerners stood on the other side and yelled for the easterners to come over and join them.

After a four-hour standoff, Checkpoint Charlie's bewildered border guards finally opened the barriers, allowing people to move freely between East and West Berlin for the first time in nearly thirty years. My assignment ended in 1987 before the wall came down.

* * *

Growing up we had guns in the house. Dad took us to fields to practice shooting on several occasions, both with a pistol and a rifle. I didn't have any problem earning a Small Arms Expert Marksmanship Ribbon during basic training by shooting the targets with an M-16 rifle. Dad taught me how to breathe correctly and to not shake the trigger. Dad was a good shooter too. He kept a loaded shotgun in the trunk of his car. Often, he displayed road rage but never pulled the rifle out of the trunk. I worried about him killing some someone during one of his rages.

When I received orders to go to Berlin Dad gave me the rifle that he kept in the trunk of his car. He thought that I would need to protect myself from the "commies." According to Dad, a "commie" believes in communism, not freedom like we have in America. He hated "commies" as much as he despised the "gooks." I thought it was better for me to have the rifle than him so I accepted the gift. I would spend less time worrying about what Dad could do with it.

I shipped the rifle to Berlin with my household goods. It took two months for it to arrive at Tempelhof Air Base. I was allowed to declare and ship the rifle to Berlin through the military but I wasn't allowed to take it back to the United States at the end of my assignment. I found this out when a crew came to pack my belongings when my tour was over.

When the packer saw the rifle he said, "This is not an item that can return to the U.S." The rifle was a beautifully wood carved old twelve-gage shotgun.

Dad was so proud of me being in the military. He loved reading the letters that I wrote from Berlin. He was excited to talk with me and asked me about my experiences when I called home every week. He bragged to his neighbors that he had a smart daughter in the military and showed them my basic training picture that he kept in his wallet.

The military gave us great opportunities to have conversations about our times serving our country and a turning point for our relationship. Abandoning his rifle made me heartsick.

I quickly figured out how to dispose of the rifle. The military police wouldn't take it. It was my problem. I gathered a bunch of foam and wrapped the rifle with rolls of duct tape around the foam. It looked like a big silver log after I finished wrapping it. I walked off the base with the unloaded duck taped packaged rifle to the Britz Canal which runs into the Spree River. I wanted to give the precious gift a safe resting place in the bottom of the canal. I figured it would just rust and be useless to anyone.

After spinning in a circle like a disc thrower and flinging the rifle from one of the ends into the air toward the canal water, the awkward package landed with a splash but didn't sink like my heart did. Instead, it started floating down the river. The package was heavy. It didn't occur to me that it wouldn't sink. I was certain that it would safely tank to the bottom of the canal. With all the foam and duct tape I created a float. The water was deep and swift so I couldn't retrieve the run-away rifle.

I can't even image the thoughts of the possible East or West German person who recovered the rifle after it floated to shore somewhere. What were they thinking when they began unraveling the shiny gray duct tape from the blue foam and discovering an antique rifle made in the U.S.A.? I'm sure that rifle could tell some moonshine stories too, if it could only talk.

* * *

While stationed in Berlin, like other military personnel, I worried that the air corridors we were protecting could be cut-off at any time by the communists and we (our military) would be prisoners of war and sent to the very concentration camps and gas chambers that we toured when we arrived at Tempelhof Air Base to begin our tour of duty.

U.S. military could only leave Berlin by three approved travel modes. I could take a hop on a military aircraft, fly commercial, or take the military train to Frankfurt, Germany. Any of these modes of travel required significant planning ahead and could be cancelled at the last minute if the military operation needed me. We always seemed to be short staffed and our first priority was covering our shifts to protect our boarders.

Tempelhof Air Base was small enough that I could walk everywhere. I didn't need a car. There were several floors above and below the ground. It was common rumor that Hitler was able to taxi his aircraft underneath the airport then travel through the underground corridors to escape through the city.

I was able to get to my dorm room, the gym, basketball court, chow hall, and work without leaving the inside of the massive underground network by traveling through these eerie mazes.

Most corridors had heavy steel doors that were unlocked for us to travel through but not all doors were accessible. We were like rats scouring through the mazes by going up and down flights of stairs and through the steel doors to avoid the gloominess and cold rain outside.

Left-Right-Left 227

I worked in a radar tower at the 6912th Electronic Security Squadron at Tempelhof Air Base. The tower was next to my dormitory room. My room faced the airplane hangar where I could watch the military aircraft come in and out for maintenance. Sometimes we left our windows open to get air but jet fuel fumes filled our rooms regardless of opening the windows or not.

While stationed at Tempelhof Air Base, I attended full time college at the University of Maryland's European Division while working as an AC&W Systems Operator. I was in my junior year of college when I arrived at the base. I took advanced classes at the U.S Army Berlin Brigade across town because Tempelhof was so small that it only offered basic college courses. I was majoring in business management.

It took me an hour to get to class and an hour to get back. Classes were three hours long. I had to hurry back to work the midnight shift after class ended. I usually didn't have time to eat on base, so I would grab a delicious wiener schnitzel (veal hotdog) from a street vendor. The chow hall was never open when I got back to the base from class. When I wasn't in class or at work I was studying or trying to sleep in a loud dormitory where you absolutely could not sleep during the day hours, even after staying up all night on a midnight shift. There was just too much going on just like a college dormitory.

I worked out at the gym when I could, but I hurt my shoulder and neck lifting weights and had to take time out from the gym for a lot of physical therapy. I was a powerlifter and competed at base competitions until the injury, which has lasted a lifetime.

Some wonder what makes you want to try so hard. For me it involved extenuating circumstances. I didn't have a car. To get to class I took two different buses and the U-Bahn (subway) then walked another mile. The nights were usually cold and rainy when I waited for the buses. I could only take classes in the evenings because of my shift schedule at work. I had to trade someone for their midnight shift while they worked my swing shift if my class fell on my swing schedule.

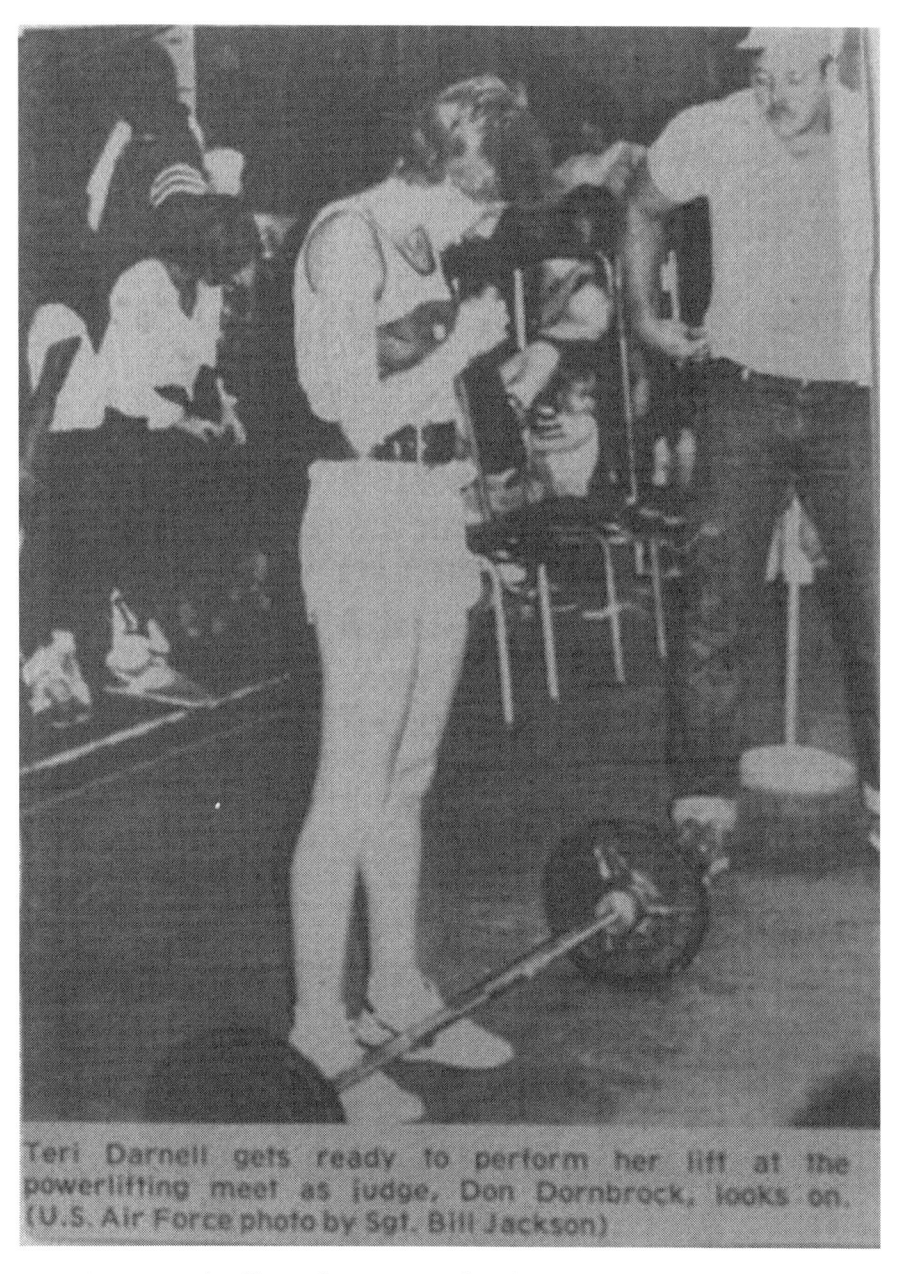

Teri Darnell gets ready to perform her lift at the powerlifting meet as judge, Don Dornbrock, looks on. (U.S. Air Force photo by Sgt. Bill Jackson)

We weren't allowed to go to school during the day because that's when a lot of the missions were performed and the busiest time at work. The big wig brass usually didn't work at night so we tracked missions during the day so they could observe.

But there was more to my work ethic than this. It was the result of growing up in a home with abuse. I was more determined than anyone I knew at the time. I was willing to work hard and sacrifice whatever it took to have a career. I was afraid to fail.

Through my letters to her, Mom was the only person I told how hard it was to work shifts and go to school full time. She'd had it hard her whole life, getting ran over by a car, having only one good leg to walk on while the other caused constant pain, having no indoor plumbing as a child, having a father that was killed on a motorcycle, having a mother that beat steal during the day and scrubbed rich people's floors on weekends. I repeated to myself, "No pain no gain" when I felt like quitting school or saying "Left-right-left, one step at a time." Mom encouraged me in her letters and weekly phone calls.

I also liked to tell Mom and Dad stories in my letters. In a letter to them dated April 8, 1984, I had my first test of taking pictures of people. I wrote, "Let me tell you this story that happened to me Friday night. I went down to Kudamm (Kurfürstendamm). It's the main shopping and entertainment strip in West Berlin. I took my camera to take pictures to send to you. I went to this one U-Bahn station (underground subway) because they have really fantastic paintings on the wall. I was in there taking pictures when I heard this German lady yelling about something I couldn't understand. I mean she was making a big deal of something. She was one of the workers cleaning in there. I thought she was yelling at another worker who was behind me. I was just standing in the subway focusing my camera trying to get a clear photo when I saw this lady through my lens running toward me, so I put my camera down from my eye still thinking she was having some do-in with another worker behind me because they were both yelling at this time.

When she was ten feet in front of me, I realized she was after me because she was giving me a look to kill. She tried to grab me and my camera. I just stood there until she was about three feet in front of me before I turned around and hauled ass up the stairs and out the door. I left her high and dry. When I turned around after I was well outside the door, I could see her with some German police. She was still yelling and screaming. By then, I was nowhere to be found. I ran as fast as I could to get away from there. It scared the shit out of me. I think I'll stay away from there for a while." That was the beginning of becoming a street photographer and really exciting.

Each Sunday afternoon, I sat by the only phone in the dormitory on our floor and waited for Mom's call. Everyone knew that 4 p.m. was my time and got off the phone when I came to claim my ten minutes of family time. We all supported each other and were respectful. We didn't have cell phones. All we had was that one phone in the hallway for personal conversations from family and friends thousands of miles away.

I aimed to get my Bachelor's degree in business management before I left Berlin and I did. The Air Force paid 75% of my tuition and I paid 25% of out-of-state tuition costs which were equivalent to paying for Florida state college tuition if I had not joined the military. I also paid for my school books. There was very little money left over to eat out or travel, but occasionally I took a trip.

* * *

I traveled to West Germany by taking the free overnight military train to Frankfurt. That was the get off point to travel anywhere else in the free world. From there I was able to get to other parts of West Germany, Holland, France, Austria and Switzerland by European trains.

Getting to Frankfurt, Germany from West Berlin required traversing through communist East Germany by a special "sealed train" known as the Frankfurt/Berlin duty train operated by the U.S. Army. No one, except U.S. and East German officials was allowed to board or exit the train at any of the checkpoints when entering or leaving East Germany. I was strictly prohibited from taking photographs, conversing with Soviet or East German guards, or even making eye contact with Soviet personnel at checkpoints while on the sealed military train.

Military trains traveled only at night, signing in at 7 p.m., departing at 8:30 p.m. with arrival in Frankfurt at 7:00 a.m. the next morning. The train traveled 115 miles through the "Iron Curtain," typically taking nine hours from point to point. If there was a problem with any military ID's or orders at the checkpoints it could take longer.

Movement orders were carefully drawn up with name, rank, and personal information copied exactly from your military identification card. Any typographical error would be grounds for refusing passage or detention by the Soviets or the East German Border Police inside Soviet East Germany.

I was always afraid that I would become a prisoner of war while traveling on the sealed train. At checkpoints no one was permitted to get off the train except for the commander, interpreter, and senior military police. The Soviet soldiers would inspect passports and orders of all the riders, which took about an hour.

Once aboard the train we could purchase snacks before entering our sleeping compartments. The beds in the military train were either equipped with four or six-person bunks. The narrow bunks with broken down thin mattresses from WWII were stacked two by two or three by three feet high on each side of the tiny six feet wide and eight feet tall compartments. The bunk beds folded down from the walls.

I didn't have a choice of who the other five bunk mates were unless I was traveling with someone. Snoring was always an option for bunk mates and crying babies occupied most women's sleeping compartments. I'm claustrophobic so when the bunks were stacked three high, I felt like a cow going to the slaughter house.

We had to stay in our bunks except to go to the toilet around the corner from the sleeping compartment. If the train was stopped at a checkpoint, we were not allowed to use the toilet because the waste landed outside on the ground. You could hear the East German guards walking around the train. When stopped we closed the curtains. Absolutely no eye contact with the commies was allowed under any circumstances. The stops at checkpoints were scary.

I usually traveled with my best friend Allen Greer, an Afro-Portuguese man. Allen became my trainer at work when I arrived at Tempelhof. We hit it off like two peas in a pod. He also took classes at night trying to get his degree in Computer Science. We took the programming language Basic together. We had to program a man entering a dark room while walking around until he found the only chair in the room to sit on. Since we were on the same work shift it was difficult for us to take the same classes since we both had to find someone to trade their midnight shift for our evening shift so we didn't miss a class.

I asked my mom if Allen could come to our house for the Christmas holiday. Mom thought it was fine but needed to check with Dad. He said no. Mom said that he didn't want the neighbors to think his daughter was dating a black man. I tried to explain that he was my best friend, not my boyfriend. It didn't matter. I was hurt that my dad cared more about what the neighbors thought of me, him, or our family than he cared for my wishes to meet my best friend who I loved dearly. I almost didn't come home.

Allen didn't have anyone to share Christmas with and I didn't want to leave him alone. I was caught between two worlds, one selfish and prejudice and the other living in a world that wasn't accepted in our society. Allen had been excommunicated from his family because he was gay, as were many of my friends in the military, kicked to the streets and homeless from religious convictions.

I realized that my mind grew and my world opened from my experiences in the military and college. I felt that my dad's mind would never expand to include people that didn't look like him or have beliefs that were not aligned with his.

When I joined the Air Force, for the first time in my life I began to understand what a narrow world I had been raised in. My dad was comfortable in his way of seeing the world and not at ease with my new beginnings. If he said black, I said white. Several times I threatened to not come home again. One was if Dad said the "n" word while I was visiting. Words can become habits of speech with no thought from the person saying it. If I heard the "n" word or others like "Fag," I felt deeply hurt. Whether the words were meant to hurt or not, I didn't want to be around people who used them.

Dad stopped saying the "n" word, at least in front of me. He'd go out of his way to tell me what nice black men he worked with at his county job on the road crew. I almost fell off my chair when he said they were not different than him.

He had no hatred for black people. He was raised to treat people of color like they were non-existent. He grew too after he worked around people different than him at the county. His mind expanded when I never thought it would. If he had been formally educated, I'm confident he'd have grown much more too, but he got his education from hard knocks and a rural upbringing.

* * *

In 1984, I traveled to Holland on a special military bus used to transport the men's and women's softball teams to play against other military bases in Europe. Usually the games were on the weekends so my boss let me off to play if there weren't any scheduled missions that required my presence.

After the Saturday game our teams ventured to the Red-Light District to see what the guys on the men's softball team kept talking up. First, the women on our team strolled by the prostitutes in the windows. The ladies were dressed in scanty clothing ready to sell themselves to onlookers. Next, we ventured into a bar to order a glass of wine. The place smelled so horribly rotten with decades of unwashed sex on the furniture that we had to leave because I started gagging.

Later in the year I went back to Amsterdam, this time with Allen. We signed up for an elective week-long class on the Life and Works of Vincent Van Gogh at the Van Gogh Museum. This class changed my life as a photographer by learning how to see and feel color. I had never been to a museum before in my life. I was fascinated by the way color was used in the painting. I studied how painters used color to bring the scenes and people to life.

We knew nothing about making reservations in advance for a hotel. As we looked around the city for a place to stay several men asked if we wanted one or two hours. I didn't understand what they were talking about in their broken English. After Allen explained it to me, we quickly moved on and had to spend a little more money for a nicer place to stay.

This voyage proved to be too expensive for coupling college credit hours with leisure traveling. After the Van Gogh class we stuck with taking the rest of our courses at the Army Brigade. We traveled to other countries when we could afford to stay in a room at someone's home. In the 1980's it was common to rent bedrooms for the night in the homes of wonderful German families for about fourteen dollars for each of our rooms. The price always included a fabulous continental breakfast with strong German coffee.

The military was a great way to see the world, get an education, and most importantly meet amazing people and form lifetime friendships. I wouldn't trade the experience for the world or the amazing friends I made like Beth Auer who I have kept in touch with for over thirty-five years.

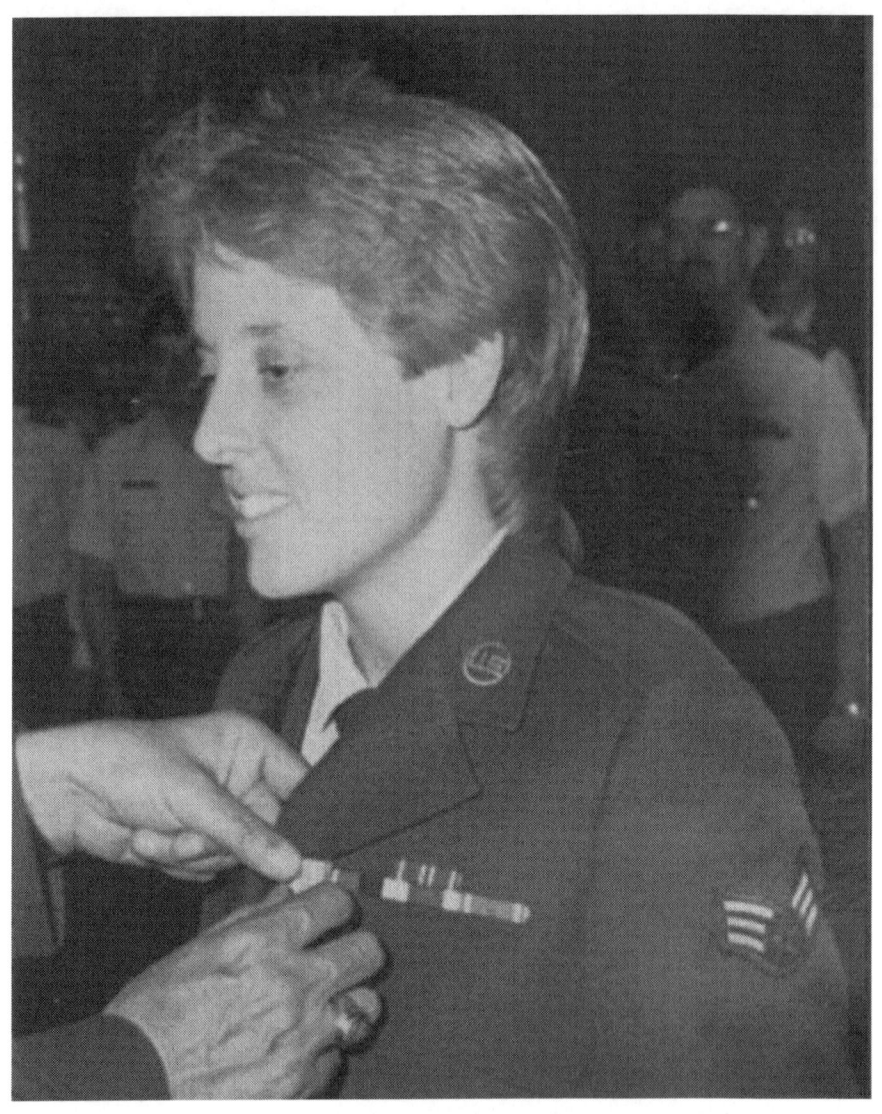

Throughout my military assignment's Mom loved and supported me with everything she was capable of giving. She was always teaching me about the ways of the world and how to cope with difficulties. She sent care packages full of goodies for all. In basic training she shipped a box of cookies and brownies for all fifty women to enjoy. We got it all over the floor and had to get it cleaned up before the technical instructor arrived. Everyone loved Mom for lifting our spirits with her unconditional love. Mom wrote letters to me with sayings like, "Never less alone than when alone" when I told her I was home sick. She sent poems and articles that helped me grow spiritually throughout my military ventures.

16

Controller

When I got out of the Air Force in 1987, I held a Bachelor's degree in Business Management, had six years of military experience, and couldn't find a job. I had to move back in with my parents in Brandon, Florida. I didn't have any money saved because I spent all that I had on college tuition and books.

The economy was in a recession. There was a spike in gas prices from the Gulf War. The surge in inflation forced the Federal Reserve to raise the discount rate to 8.00%. GDP growth and job creation remained weak. Unemployment was on the rise. Approximately 1.6 million jobs were shed during this recession. I didn't have enough money to live on. I took my calculator to the grocery store and I added every item one at a time before placing them in the shopping cart. When I got to the register to check out, I prayed that I didn't make a mistake and embarrass myself by having to retract groceries that were already rung up from lack of funds. It pained me to go to the grocery store but it pained me even more to not eat.

Out of desperation I took a job as a manager of Ponderosa Steak House in Brandon, Florida making $19,000 a year. I worked twelve hours a day, six days a week with Monday off unless it was a holiday, then I got Tuesday off.

After I closed the restaurant at night, counted all the money, performed an inventory like counting each and every steak in the freezer and refrigerator, and created a plan for the next day, I had to deposit a sack of about $3,000 in cash into the bank's outside deposit box each night at one o'clock in the morning. A year after I left the steak house job, the manager was robbed and murdered for the cash while making the nightly deposit.

When an Air Force friend called to let me know about a job opening for a Training Manager at Batch Air, Inc. at the Miami International Airport, I packed my bags and moved.

I had attended technical school to learn how to develop training programs while in the military. I developed course work and taught classes for the unit's electronic security operations while in Berlin.

Batch Air, Inc. overhauled and repaired jet engines for companies like Midway and Eastern Airlines. There was a new Federal requirement for airline mechanics to properly handle hazardous materials, but there was no training program to teach employees how to follow the regulations. I wrote a grant proposal asking the State of Florida for funds to create a Hazardous Material Handling and Disposal training program. The state gave Batch Air, Inc. ten grand for me to create the program. The state used my program as a model for future Hazardous Material training within in the state of Florida.

I also developed other technical training materials for repairing jet engines and taught the mechanics at Batch Air how to follow the required procedures. I employed an interpreter because most mechanics didn't read, write or speak English.

I found that the training development process was slow and ineffective, since it used paper-based materials, so I created a new and uncommon type of video training for the mechanics. The owner of the company purchased a camcorder for me. I filmed an expert performing every tedious procedure for repairing jet engines. I documented the procedures on film and created a library so Spanish speaking mechanics could follow the FAA regulations for repairing engines. I was promoted to the Director of Training position and received an additional ten thousand dollars a month for my creative ideas and innovative techniques.

* * *

While living in Miami I drove to Brandon once a month to visit Mom and Dad on weekends. It was only a four-hour drive. Dad worked for the county transportation department operating heavy equipment. He had a day time job and steady income for a change. He seemed to stay in pretty good spirits and had lots of friends in the neighborhood. The neighbors gathered every evening in Mom and Dad's garage to "shoot the shit" and drink Old Milwaukee beer. Dad always had a refrigerator full of beer.

During a weekend in Brandon when I was twenty-seven years old, I was across the street at Mom and Dad's neighbor's house. It was getting dark outside when I walked back to my parent's house. Out of nowhere I was pinched hard on the ass. I immediately threw my elbow into the man's gut. I spun around and kneed him hard in the balls. A man dropped to the ground holding his penis and whimpered like a baby. I was surprised to see my parents' age neighbor lying in their front yard in the fetal position. Danny ran toward me to see if I was alright. He was across the street (where I came from) and witnessed the series of assaults.

As a result of the sexual assault experience I had in the military at Homestead AFB, I was always on guard about being attacked from behind. I reacted to the hard pinch before having a chance to think. He went down hard and fast. When Dan found out that I was OK, he laughed his ass off at the dirty old man and told him not to mess with his big sister.

Word got around the neighborhood about incident. Most of the men stayed clear of me after that, except Harry Brown. I loved Harry and his wife Linda. Harry owned a business fixing small appliance motors by rewiring the copper inside the motor. Linda kept Harry's business books and prepared tax returns for extra money.

Harry and Linda always encouraged me to work hard and have fun at it. I enjoyed their positive energy and unconditional love and support. They were good neighbors and a great influence for our family.

Harry loved Coo Coo clocks. When I was stationed in Berlin, I took the duty train and traveled eighteen hours to the Black Forest to buy him a genuine Coo Coo clock. He gave me the money for it. I loved the adventure.

* * *

Dad got into an accident at work. He fell off the top of a back hoe while climbing the ladder to enter the cab. He landed on his back. Over time he had two back surgeries and could no longer operate the heavy equipment. The pill pushing doctors prescribed lots of pain killers. He became addicted to them and coupled the pills with alcohol, a lethal combination for his instability. He stocked up on Darvocet's and gave away pills like candy to relatives who came to visit. Later he was prescribed OxyContin when Darvocet's were banned for causing heart attacks.

One weekend while I was visiting, Dad took too many pain pills and got drunk too. I had ignorantly assumed that life was better for them and that he had stopped the beatings because he seemed happy. I had hoped that the Florida sunshine was offering them a better life than they had when Dad was a truck driver and gone all the time. I didn't really know for sure because I was away in the military and not present to keep an eye on Mom. Mom never expressed unhappiness in her letters. She was too busy giving me encouragement. She never asked for any help for herself.

That night Dad was drugged, drunk, angry, and dangerous. I could hear him accusing Mom of sleeping with the neighbor who pinched my ass. He starting beating her and the screaming began. I immediately went into the bedroom and demanded he stop. I had grown up and became strong and fearless. I told him if I ever witnessed or heard about him hitting her again that I would kill him. I meant it. I wanted to kill him then, but I didn't. He sobered up and knew how much I meant it. He cried and cried promising me that it would never happen again. That night he became afraid of me and I lost my fear of him. The next day I drove back to Miami for work.

* * *

Soon, I saw the writing on the wall for Batch Air, Inc. Rumors were flying that Midway and Eastern Airlines were in financial trouble and expected to go out of business. I started thinking about another career but the economy was in economic shambles and unemployment rates were high again.

I made a lot of contacts working in the transportation field at Miami's International Airport. I found out that the Federal Aviation Administration (FAA) was in desperate need of Air Traffic Controllers as a result of the 1981 union strike that sought better working conditions and pay. By striking the union violated U.S Code 5 which prohibits strikes by federal government employees. President Ronald Reagan declared the strike a "peril to national safety" and ordered the controllers back to work under the terms of the Taft-Hartley Act.

Only 1,300 of the nearly 13,000 controllers returned to work, so Regan demanded that the others forfeit their position if they didn't return to work with forty-eight hours. Regan fired the 11,345 striking air traffic controllers who ignored the order and banned them from federal service for life.

In the wake of the strike and mass firings, the FAA was faced with the task of hiring and training enough controllers to replace the fired ones. At the time it took three years in normal conditions to train a new controller. The FAA had initially claimed that staffing levels would be restored within two years. It took closer to a decade before the overall staffing levels returned to normal.

I applied for the Air Traffic Controller position and was hired as a trainee. I traveled to the FAA Academy in Oklahoma City for three months of school. In the initial four-week period we learned about the basics of navigation. We also had to memorize climb and ground speeds for about fifty aircraft types and their three-letter FAA codes.

Then we had to memorize and draw a detailed map of the airport training area without using any notes. I scored almost 100% on all the academic tests. As training moved on to the practical phases, we began to learn the art of keeping airplanes moving in an orderly manner and separated in space.

Each simulation was graded and a constant source of stress. The simulations consisted of a brief setup period where we accessed fifteen flight strips and formed a mental plan for how best handle the next simulation. Any error, even if immediately caught and corrected, resulted in points deducted from our score.

To become an AC&W Operator in the military I had to pass a depth perception test administered with an eye exam. I failed the eye test because I couldn't see 3D. I was given a waiver and was able to perform the AC&W job using the radar scope without a problem. But as an Air Traffic Controller I needed that 3D skill because we didn't use a radar scope while in training.

During the final simulation we were required to control fifteen aircraft using only the data on the flight strips. The information on the strips had to be memorized instantaneously. The instructors kept throwing in emergency situations and there was no time to relook at flight strips during the simulation.

We had to control the aircraft with a vision inside our head. We had to land aircraft in distress and avoid crashing into the distressed one with the other fourteen aircraft that were circling or in a holding pattern. Before one aircraft was out of distress another one was starting having a disaster. It was like juggling fifteen balls in the air and you couldn't let any ball hit the ground or all the people in the airplane would die.

I was the best in the class on all the academic training but I couldn't get the hang of controlling without a radar scope. If the electricity went off and all the generators failed in real life, the people in the aircraft under my command would die because I couldn't see in 3D. I quit. This was the first time in my life that I failed at anything at which I had tried so hard to succeed. It was at one of the lowest points of my life. I was homeless.

I was too embarrassed to go back home to Florida. I felt like a failure. I asked Mom's sister if I could stay with her for a couple months until I found a job and a place to live. I headed to Cleveland defeated, deflated and "without a pot to piss in."

17

Career

In the desolate economy during the fall of 1989 everywhere I applied for a job in Cleveland, Ohio touted the same line, "we're not hiring." The World Wide Web didn't become publicly available until 1991 to make it easier to find information. I searched through classified ads in Cleveland's Plain Dealer newspaper, postings at the public library, and any job available at the unemployment office. I wasn't eligible for unemployment because I quit my Air Traffic Controller training position with the FAA. I submitted resumes to the few management positions advertised in the newspaper.

In desperation I applied for an hourly wage typing job through the Manpower temporary agency. They gave me a typing test and politely told me that I would probably be better suited for another type of career.

Manpower informed me that United Parcel Service was looking for temporary help during the upcoming Christmas season. In the Air Force I had learned how to drive a standard shift five-ton truck. I knew that driving a UPS package car wouldn't be a problem. I was also in top shape from running and lifting weights. I thought this would be the perfect job for me. I was beyond motivated to do it. Minimum wage for the typing job that I didn't get was $3.35 an hour. As a trainee for UPS the delivery job started at $7 an hour. The pay was less than I made at Batch Air, Inc. but the company had potential for me to get into management since I had a bachelor's degree in business management and military experience that seemed valued by UPS.

Manpower informed me to go to the Human Resources office in Middleburg Heights, a suburb of Cleveland. I immediately drove to the office and filled out an application. I was told that they wouldn't be interviewing until late October but they would keep my application on file. My heart sank.

It was early October and I was running out of savings. I made it my new job for UPS to hire me. I got the hiring manager's name and phone number while in the office. I left a voice mail on Nancy Frank's office telephone voice recorder everyday letting her know that I was ready for work. I went to the UPS hiring office three times a week to make sure they remembered me. I let them know that I was checking in and ready to help.

I learned a lot about UPS' hiring process as I stood around watching the lines of people applying for the scarce amount of driving positions they had to fulfill. I wanted the driving position, not the part-time loading job that seemed to be more readily available.

When I was called in for an interview, I wore a nice navy-blue business suit with a white shirt, skirt and heels. I wanted UPS to know that they weren't just hiring a driver. They would be hiring a potential management person with experience that lined up with the company's values.

I didn't know any other woman who would want this type of job. I believed that I was a perfect fit. I went to the library and learned everything I could about UPS. For every interview question I had a positive professional answer. The only thing that I had going against me was that I had only lived the Cleveland area for a couple months. They were worried about me leaving. I assured Nancy that Cleveland was my new home. I got the job.

Three days before Christmas when delivery volume was at its peak, the temperature got down to minus fifteen degrees in Cleveland, not counting the wind chill factors.

I was required to record every delivery stop on a paper form with carbon paper underneath so there would be an extra copy. When I tried to write on the form the frozen pen would tear the paper. I had to put the tip of the pen inside my mouth until the ink thawed and would write.

A thin wooded clipboard held the stack of paper forms. The clipboard was also used to swat dogs that jumped out of people's front door to bite my ankles or calves. I ran up and down driveways as fast as I could go while slipping and sliding on the ice and snow to stay warm.

It wasn't until 1991 that UPS invented the handheld Delivery Information Acquisition Device (DIAD). The DIAD replaced the paper method of logging stops. It was developed to capture and upload delivery information to the UPS network. This technological efficiency eliminated the use of 59 million sheets of paper, equal to more than five thousand trees per year. I trained the first drivers to use the DIAD. The union made a big deal out of the new technology and wanted drivers to be paid as computer operators instead of truck drivers. It turned out that UPS drivers made more money than computer operators. As a driver in 1990 I earned $21,000 for only nine months of employment and that was on the low end of the pay scale because I was a new driver.

During Christmas season in 1989 I about froze my ass off. There wasn't any heat inside the package car that could be felt with the doors open while traveling stop-to-stop. It took too long to open and close the doors during peak season at UPS. Time was critical to get an average of three hundred and fifty stops delivered each day. The truck was so full in the morning that the only way to get into the back was to crack the bulkhead door, reach for a package stuffed in the isle, grap it with hopes that nothing else would fall into the cabin area until I could make room to sort things out and get on schedule.

I hustled just like running line drills in basketball practice, except I did these deliveries ten to twelve hours a day carrying up to seventy pounds up and down long driveways on Lake Avenue. Often if I delivered a QVC package, the next day I was back at that same house picking it up and taking it back to the UPS package center for its return to QVC. As I ran up the driveways, I only imagined what the husbands had to say about their wives watching QVC all day. It was always the same houses getting the stuff and returning it the next day. This was before online shopping and the beginning for UPS to gear up for massive retail deliveries to homes.

After the Christmas peak season was over, I was terminated as a temporary package car driver. I was given hope by the management team that I could be called back and offered a full-time driver's job in the spring of 1990 when the package volume returned. It was complicated. To fill a union driving job, UPS was required to hire three people from inside the company first, then one person from outside the company next. I was an outsider. In the spring, the center manager concluded that the next one and only permanent driving job that became available in the district would be filled by an outside person. They offered the job to me. I was the only woman out of the ten temporary drivers hired for the entire district of North Ohio that Christmas season. I was elated to begin a new career at a great company. To get that one and only job, I had to go far beyond what was expected of me.

For example, during peak season temporary drivers called in to see if they'd get to work that day. If the center had enough volume, they'd take splits off other package cars to build enough volume for a temporary driver to have an eight-hour driving day. I lived with my aunt in Elyria and it was a forty-five-minute drive to the hub. I learned quickly that if they called me in, I needed to be there and ready to drive within fifteen minutes. Instead of calling to see if they had enough work for me, I drove to the center every morning and waited for work. While waiting, I stepped into the offices and watched the management team plan and put out fires.

UPS operations are chaotic during Christmas season. I found this chaos exciting and asked lots of questions when the supervisor's time permitted. I observed. I wanted to be part of the team and started laying the path to get there. For the first time in my life I knew that I had found a home and planned to stay. I drove a package car for a year, learned most every route the in the Westlake center in the Middleburg Heights district as a swing driver, then was promoted into management as an Industrial Engineer.

For two years, I took time studies of drivers on their routes by counting the steps they took to walk from place to place and documenting every move they made on a form that was later key entered into a computer to determine the allotted amount of time needed for the driver's route.

My manager, Josie Matusik taught me how important it was to ensure complete accuracy of the drivers' routes for fairness to the driver and for the cost to UPS. She was a master at teaching us about processes and procedures in extraordinary detail. She told me to not come to her with a problem, but a solution. So, anytime I had a problem, I told her how I was going to fix it. She always provided advice if I was off track on the solution. I stuck with this advice for the rest of my career. My time study team was the first and only team in UPS History to get a 100% rating on a National Time Study audit through her leadership.

My team was assigned to measure the routes in hardcore union Akron, Ohio. In this area, drivers hated time study people. One driver told me that the last time study person took five minutes off his route for getting the job done. He told me that five minutes meant five hundred dollars stolen out of his pocket each year. Other than that, he hardly said a word. This particular guy helped me build patience while he tested my character.

The driver tried to intimidate me by pulling up to a dumpster behind a convenient store. He instructed me to go dig for my lunch while he whipped out his paper bag full of snacks and sandwiches for himself. This didn't faze me. During my life every time Dad passed a garbage truck when we drove in the car he would yell out, "There goes your lunch bucket." He thought it was funny. I found no humor in it. As far as the smart-ass driver, I didn't need lunch. I knew how to survive without it, no problem. Been there many times before.

The driver didn't want to listen to anything about how routes change when strip malls take over residential areas. It takes three steps to get inside an outdoor strip mall retail store versus fifty steps to walk up a long driveway to make a delivery. Do the math. Less steps, less money.

After the final data analysis, it was time to review the results with each driver in the center that was time studied. During the review with the hard-core ass-hole, I heard enough four-letter words and derogatory statements that I left the office after the fifteen-minute review to talk with the union steward. From my point of view, the driver didn't have grounds for an appeal. The minus ten minutes stuck for the new route time. I knew with 100% certainty that the time study was flawless. I prepared ahead and had a plan to combat the wrath of the driver.

You didn't sit around and pout or complain about assholes. Like in the military, you can't show weakness, especially in a male dominated company like UPS, or you will be eaten alive. What I did learn from my beloved Chief Master Sergeant of the Air Force in Berlin, David King, was that there was "power of the pen." And, "that you get far more with sugar than vinegar." That driver was full of piss and vinegar and maybe he learned a lesson from my power of the pen, but I doubt it. He's probably still stewing over it.

During another time study, I met driver that I adored. UPS didn't have a shirt big enough to fit him. He kept popping the buttons and exposing his "jelly belly." UPS typically hires skinny wiry types that move with speed and diligence, not overweight people. I doubted this guy could move at all. He timed the stops perfectly on his route that had several public schools.

The cooks at the schools accepted the deliveries in the kitchen. In turn, they provided the driver with a hot plate of food. He scurried back to the package car after the delivery with his hands full of a plate of cafeteria food, and he scarfed the breakfast down as he briskly walked while his belly jiggled.

Throughout the day the driver repeated over and over again, "This fat boy can move, this fat boy can move" while laughing, sweating, breathing deeply, and expelling air out like thunder. And he could move without a doubt. The whole vehicle shook as he jumped into the driver's seat to take off grinding the gears all the way down the road in the shiny brown 1960's P600 package car.

* * *

While working in UPS operations, something kept nagging at me to go back to school at night, like it wasn't hard enough the first time. In letters to Mom from Berlin, I mentioned that I wanted to get a Master's Degree in Business Administration (MBA) when finished with my bachelor's degree. I put that idea aside for a few years because I didn't have the money to pay for it.

In 1993, I took a lateral position at UPS as an Employee Relations Supervisor in Human Resources. I wanted to save the world but mostly pushed a lot of papers around which wasn't mentally challenging. Occasionally, I actually talked with employees. I got assigned to work in the same hard-core union center in Akron, Ohio that I had time studied.

The Division Manager was a real jerk. One day while getting ready to teach a class I walked by a group of people near the classroom door. I over-heard an Operations Manager tell an African American man that he looked just like the statue he had in his front yard. I was shocked. The young man was a part-time package loader. I walked up to the loader and profusely apologized for the ignorant manager's behavior. The manager took off. I found the Division Manager and told him what happened. He was not pleased with my story. He didn't seem a bit upset about the manager's unacceptable, discriminatory, inflammatory, disparaging remarks. He was mad that he would have to do something about it.

The next day the bigot Operations Manager was moved to a similar job, except at night dispatching long haul trucks where there didn't appear to be any African American workers.

I got indirectly punished for reporting the incident. The next day, the Division Manager brought me into his office and told me to move all my sensitive information human resources files and cabinets out of my office into the hallway next to his office because he decided that would be my new office, the hallway next to the men's room where people walked through to the break room. He said he needed my office for the pre-load management team who worked the midnight to 9 am shift.

UPS had a program called Talk, Listen, and Action (TLA). One of my job responsibilities entailed talking with each part-time employee in the building, listening to anything they had to say, and documenting the conversation on a form. The form was tracked at the Region level. It was a mandatory UPS program.

After the discussion, I researched the employee's issues and got back with them with answers, usually benefits related. The conversation was designed to be held in a closed-door office where employees felt free to express their issues or opinions with confidentiality. After I lost my office, I attempted to have TLA's in the break room, but union employees complained that I was using their break space as an office. The Division Manager told me that all future TLA's would be done at the package car or trailer where the employees loaded and unloaded, and that I was not to stop their production while talking with them.

While performing a TLA with an employee loading a trailer, I had to stand above them on a cat walk. The cat walk had a see-through grate. In 1994, UPS women were not allowed to wear pants. We had to "Dress for Success." We watched a mandatory video of what we were and were not allowed to wear to work. An acceptable professional management ward robe for a woman included a skirt, blouse, jacket, neutral pantyhose, and black or brown pumps, even in operations.

Because of the exceptionally loud noise inside a package operation where belts and cages are moving in all directions, I yelled through the metal grate so the loader could hear my questions. He tried not to stare straight up my skirt, but it couldn't be helped. It was embarrassing and humiliating for both of us. I learned to put on shorts under my skirt when conducting a TLA with a loader. The conversation was anything but confidential as other loaders tried to ease drop.

I was one of very few women on the management team in Akron and not given any support by the men, especially the Division Manager. He set me up to get me to quit because I spoke up about discrimination. Again, I had to grit and grind my teeth to survive. I needed a change.

* * *

I learned that UPS would pay 100% of my college tuition if I wanted to go back to school for an MBA. Uncovering that information was like finding gold at the end of the rainbow. I could hardly believe that almost nobody took advantage of the benefit. Could it be because we worked fifty-five hours a week already? I felt like I needed to be a step above everyone else as a security blanket for employability based on my last effort of not being able to get a management job in a downward economy with a bachelor's degree in business. I couldn't even get a minimum wage typing job. UPS gave me a chance and I was going to make it successful.

Luckily, I got out of Akron and worked as an Employment Center Supervisor at the Middleburg Heights hub so I could go back to school.

I enrolled at Baldwin Wallace University's Executive MBA weekend program and graduated after eighteen months with a 3.95 GPA. Baldwin Wallace was located near the Middleburg Heights operations hub. The location made it faster for me to get from work to the late Friday afternoon classes. The convenient location prompted me to pick that school even though the tuition cost was higher because it was a private Methodist college.

At the end of the program I was so burnt out that I opted out of taking a final test and got an A- in the marketing course. I graduated from high school a year early and received my diploma in the mail. I also received my Bachelor's degree diploma in the mail from the University of Maryland's European Division.

For my first and only stage graduation my entire family (granny, Mom, Dad, brothers, sister-in-law, niece, and nephew) piled in Mom and Dad's 1990 red four-door Cadillac Deville and navigated up Hillbilly Highway to attend my college graduation after picking up granny in Kentucky. They drove twenty-one hours to come to the graduation ceremony. I loved sharing that time with my family.

Soon after I graduated, UPS moved its headquarters from Greenwich, Connecticut to Atlanta, Georgia and needed Marketing Analysts with MBA's. I interviewed for the position and was offered the job. I relocated to Atlanta a year before the 1996 Olympics to be closer to my family.

A few years after I moved to Atlanta, UPS consolidated districts in the United States. The North Ohio district office where I worked near Cleveland was absorbed into Central Ohio's regional operations in Columbus. Most of the staff people in the Cleveland offices were terminated. An angel watched over me and pushed me to go back to school to get the MBA. Otherwise, I would have been without a job again and "without a pot to piss in."

18

End

As an adult, I didn't spend much time with Dennis Jr. When I graduated from high school, I joined the military. Dennis Jr. got married and started having kids. Before he got married, he was the manager of a rock band in Brandon, Florida and loved to party with his friends. He worked for Otis installing elevators in high rise buildings in Tampa. He started the job pretty quickly out of high school and worked his way up to foreman. When a position became available allowing him to have a service route on the Pan Handle of Florida, he moved his family to Freeport. He enjoyed being outdoors. Living in Freeport provided Dennis Jr. freedom to fish and hunt.

Mom and Dad followed Dennis Jr. and his family to Freeport. They bought a house with a pond full of ducks, geese, and a couple alligators. Every day one goose strutted from the pond to their back porch. If Dad was sitting outside in the lawn chair it would jump up, sit on his lap, and peck at the buttons on his shirt. They began bonding when the goose was a baby. Dad tossed the goose bread in the yard as they strolled around together. Dad loved animals. He didn't have a need to be jealous of them.

Mom and Dad didn't know Dennis Jr. was drinking too much. I didn't suspect that he had a problem with alcohol and drugs. He always seemed happy and was an exceptionally hard worker, never missing a day of work. He began partying hard with the rock band and didn't quit that lifestyle after getting married and having two kids.

I got a call July 18, 1998 at 2 a.m. from my sister-in-law. Dennis Jr. wrecked his car. He was driving an old hunting jeep on a dark two-lane road near his house. He hit the side of a small bridge that crossed a creek. The jeep flipped in mid-air landing on top of him and his passenger, killing them both. He was thirty-nine years old and survived by his wife and two young children. We will never know exactly what happened, but Dennis Jr. was drinking and driving.

Dad lost his Dad at a young age and so did Mom. Now my niece and nephew lost their Dad, my parents lost their son, and Dan and I lost our big brother. All these accidents were avoidable. Devastation crippled us.

After a couple of years Mom and Dad moved back to the Tampa Bay area to Sun City Center, Florida. They couldn't stay in Freeport any longer from the horrific memories of the accident that surrounded them. The kids were young teenagers and rarely visited so they left.

Dad didn't show his ugly side to his grand kids. He loved them dearly. He had nicknames for them to: "Piss Willy, Piss Ant and Piss Lucy." That's what he called them since birth. He had nicknames for relatives too. He called my cousin David "kidarette." Dad would go to my aunt and uncles house in Wurtland, Kentucky and smoke cigarettes on the front porch then flick the cigarette butt into the side yard. David would run out the back door, sneak around the side when they weren't looking, grab the butt and smoke it. He's been smoking since.

* * *

Mom and Dad moved to a retirement community in Sun City Center, Florida on the south end of Tampa. They lived on a golf course that had a small retention pond. Dad didn't play golf but he loved the Sand Hill Cranes that hung out near the pond. The cranes came by their house daily and pecked on the glass door to let him know they were there to be fed. He named one of the cranes Knot Neck because it had a tumor on the side of its neck. He basked in glory when the birds came to visit. They ate right out of his hand. The birds made his day, every day. Dad was always happy around animals.

In 2002, Dad took up an old hobby flying small airplanes. He had a student pilot license and rented an old Cessna Skyhawk single engine airplane near their home at Wimauma Air Park Airport. This gave him something constructive to do and it got him out of the house for a while instead of sitting on the couch watching "shoot 'em ups" as Mom called the old westerns. They bought a house where there was a wall separating the kitchen from the living room so Mom didn't have to be in the middle of the "shoot 'em ups." Not everyone wants the modern open concept home, definitely not Mom.

Dad had a way of constantly annoying Mom by hollering out, "Carol, where's the blah blah blah?" even if it was the TV remote lying on the table next to him. He barely did a thing for himself after the accident where he fell off the backhoe.

Dad enjoyed socializing with old cronies having similar interests at the airport. Renting airplanes by the hour became too expensive so he ordered an ultralight aircraft kit off the internet for a mere three thousand dollars. Mom, the take back queen, couldn't take that purchase back because there was no refund.

The Sun City Center Community Association had fifty pages of Conditions, Covenants and Restrictions about what you can't have or do with the property you own. Not one word was mentioned about having an ultralight airplane in your front yard. As long as the airplane didn't reside in the yard overnight there was nothing the association or the neighbors could do about Dad's new hobby.

He built the aircraft one section at a time out of the hot sun inside the sweltering garage. When it was time to assemble and paint the aircraft, he dragged the sections to the driveway and began to piece the ultralight together. The manicured front yard turned bright yellow from the south easterly winds blowing the spray paint on every flat surface.

My uncle Monty accompanied Dad on the yellow canary's first voyage to Wimauma Air Park. Monty is Dad's half-brother on his mother's side. Monty grew up in Michigan, a completely different culture than Dad's upbringing in Appalachia. He and Dad butted heads all the time, but so did Dad and I. Monty didn't get Dad's silly or obnoxious jokes. He was much more serious than Dad but seemed to ignore most of Dad's shortcomings because they were half-brothers.

Monty and his wife Marge are members the Seventh Day Adventist church. When Monty challenged Dad's views of the world, Dad called him a 'Pot Licker' and a 'bible thumper'. Dad didn't know how to verbally make a persuasive argument to defend attacks on his beliefs; instead he would get mad, call names, or be ready to fist fight to defend his character.

The wings of the yellow canary were removable so they could be toted down the road to the airfield on a trailer with the rest of the canary yellow ultralight. According to Dad, he trailered the aircraft to the airfield where he and Uncle Monty unloaded it near the runway and hooked the wings on. Dad was not a test pilot and only had a student pilot license to operate an airplane, but one doesn't need a license to fly an experimental aircraft such as an ultralight. You just need to be a little crazy.

Dad taxied the aircraft up and down the runway. He flew the canary a few feet above the ground to make sure the parts were secure and the engine was running properly. When he became confident that all was intact, he set off for the brilliant blue sky.

After climbing to six hundred feet in the air, Dad tried to turn the aircraft back to the runway when the aileron stuck. He couldn't get the lever to release the tension. An aileron (French for "little wing" or "fin") is a hinged flight control surface usually forming part of the trailing edge of each wing of a fixed-wing aircraft. Airplanes use ailerons in pairs to control the rolls and banks.

Dad's ultralight began rolling and banking then taking a nose dive toward the ground. As it crashed into the tomato field it pitched Dad out the front window before securing a position with the tail straight up while the cockpit absorbed the fresh tomatoes. When Dad was tossed out the window he bounced and rolled twenty feet in the soft dirt that had been recently plowed. According to my uncle, a man came out to the field and started yelling at Dad and my uncle because the crashing aircraft extracted some of his tomato plants.

The tomato grower demanded immediate payment as he screamed at Dad who was lying in the dirt for ruining part of his crop. Dad was medevacked to Tampa General Hospital and only suffered scrapes, cuts, and bruises, just like the time he tried to kill himself on the motorcycle as he smashed though boards with his chest.

A few months after the plane crash, I discovered a letter size manila envelope in my mailbox with a return address of Carol Darnell. When I opened the envelop there was nothing inside except the picture of Dad laid out in the dirt looking dead in front of his upside-down canary yellow plane in a field of tomatoes. Monty took the picture at the crash site and gave it to Mom and Dad. This was Moms cry for help that I didn't absorb or realize. She never asked for help. I had no idea visual evidence existed of this near disaster until Mom sent the picture. I was too busy with my career at UPS to absorb Mom's subtle plea.

Dad had t-shirts made with the crash picture on it. He was proud of being a survivor and told the airplane story to anyone who would listen. He insisted that anyone who came to the house watch on his TV the recorded local new channel's coverage of the plane crash. Now, he was an infamous seventy-one-year-old man claiming his fame thereby making Mom a nervous wreck because she had to constantly relive the fear of the accident.

* * *

In 2005, Dad gave his old Isuzu Rodeo to my nephew. My nephew wrecked his car and didn't have the money to buy another one. Now my parents were down to one car. Dad would take off every day in Mom's 1998 white Oldsmobile with a blue cloth hardtop. The front bumper was all scratched up from Mom scraping off the love bugs with a green scour pad then attempting to paint the bumper with white house trim paint.

The big ass car was perfect for Sun City Center. You need a solid car because ninety-year-old women and men drive on the wrong side of the road. When you get behind one going the maximum thirty miles an hour on Del Webb road, you can't see their heads through the back window from hunching over the steering wheel to see ahead. The old cars looked like they drove themselves.

Mom's had a few people tail end her Oldsmobile. A big box Coke truck parked in the regular lot backed into her rear bumper at the local Public grocery store. In the same parking lot, one old woman stepped on the gas instead of the brake and landed in the retention pond. Finally, Public put up a guard rail after that swimming lesson. Luckily a perimetric snatched her out before the alligators got her.

Mom had her daily routine of picking up medications from Public, shopping for food, going to the library, all the stuff you need to do to run a household with someone who does nothing but watch westerns on TV. Now she didn't have a car.

She told Dad when she needed the car and he took off anyway. This was the first time that I received a direct call from Dad, ever, and I was at work. He said Mom wanted a divorce. I have never heard the big "D word" come out of either of their mouths before. After speaking with both of them and asking lots of questions, it seemed the problem had a simple solution…get another car.

They bought a 2005 gold Cadillac Seville from a retired cop. Dad counted out the many one hundred-dollar bills and handed them over to the slippery ex-cop. The cop casually mentioned that the fancy pants car had a slight oil leak after he had the money in his hands. But the Cadillac looked pretty, had heated and cooled leather seats, and everything operated with a push of a button so Dad had to have it, an American car, the American Dream. Mom wanted a Toyota.

Before the Cadillac purchase, Mom finally got Dad to look at a Camry on a dealership lot. She was ready to make the purchase. Dad drove her around to the back of the lot and screamed at her and berated her until she was shaken with grief. This time he didn't hit her, but she wasn't getting that Toyota, not over his dead body.

The Cadillac leaked oil in the garage and in the driveway, one drip at a time. It just about drove Mom crazy. The oil was messing up her carpeted garage and beautiful stone driveway. Mom likes things clean and neat, not oily and leaky. They took the car to the dealership to get an estimate for repairing the leak. It was three thousand dollars to replace a seal where the whole damn thing had to be taken apart to get to it. They kept the car but didn't fix the leak. At least they had a second car now.

In Dad's eyes, he didn't need to get the Cadillac inspected before purchasing it, ignoring Moms and my advice. Dad trusted the crusty old retired cop. Dad thought a police officer would be honest. Well he was, sort of, after he had the cash in his hands. They got screwed, but should have known better. It's still dripping oil on the pile of Tampa Tribunes stacked on top of the carpet and under the car today.

Mom's luck remained the same the time the Electrolux man came knocking on the door to sell vacuum cleaners. Dad sold them in Wheelersburg for a couple of weeks and nobody bought one except for our family at a discount. He had a soft spot for the salesman. This time, they bought the deluxe upright model for $2500.

The steel tank of the vacuum cleaner also cleans furniture (maybe even toilets) and weighs too much for Mom to push around the house with her bad leg. It sits in the bedroom closet and has never been used. Between the airplane, the Cadillac, and the vacuum, thousands of dollars were flying out the door. They didn't have a plan if something happened to either one of them. The plan has always been no plan, ride by the seat of your pants, no life insurance, no savings, no investments, no plan, period.

*   *   *

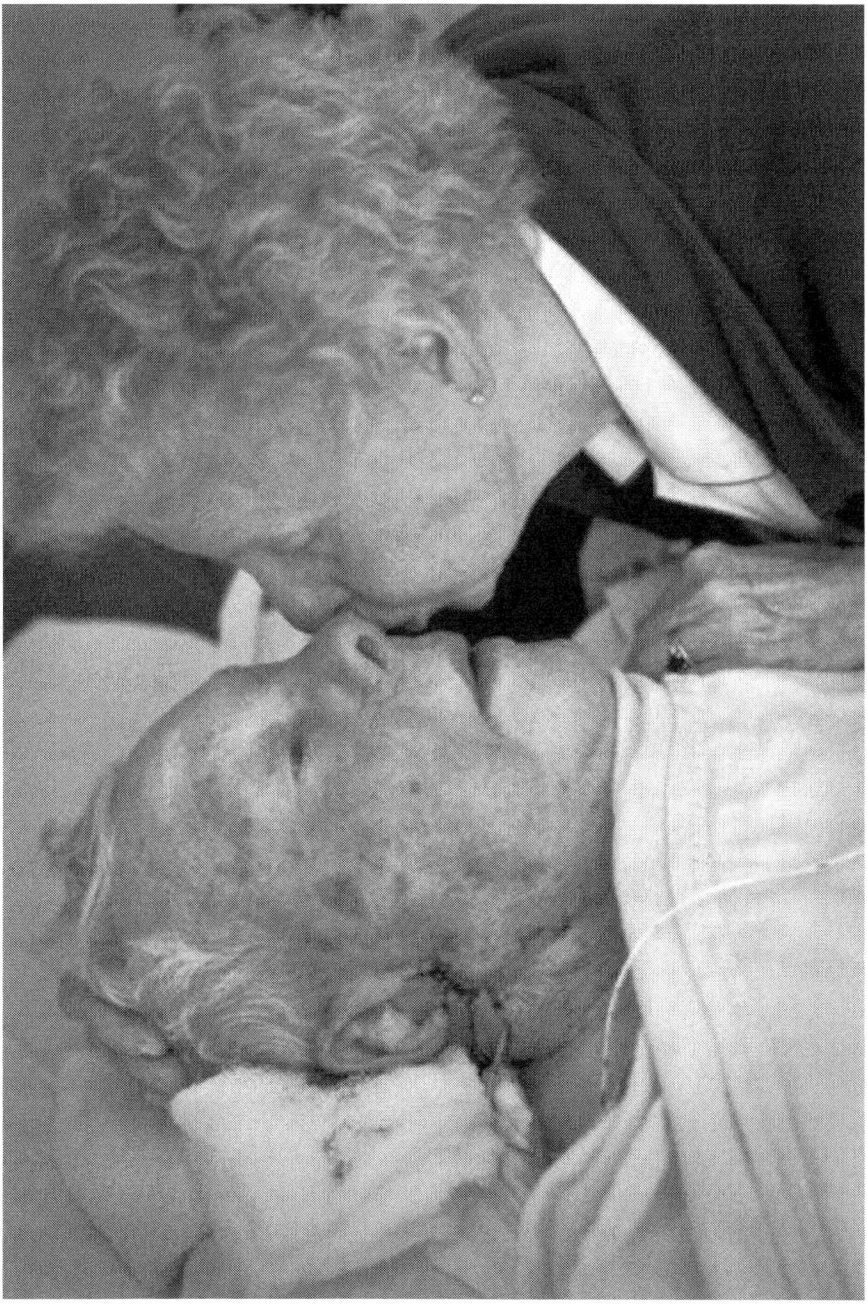

In 2008, Dad was diagnosed with a large malignant tumor in his neck near the ear canal. The tumor was removed along with the bottom half of his ear, like Van Gogh. Mom took him to dozens of chemotherapy and radiation treatments in Brandon, twenty miles away. Dad couldn't drive to the appointments. He constantly yelled at her while she was driving the Cadillac. Turn here...turn there..., it made her shake.

In his eyes she couldn't do anything right. All he had to do was show up to the dinner table, eat, and leave his dishes laying there. She did everything to run the house and take care of him. She was worn out completely. Mom went into a deep depression and lost forty pounds in a few months. She weighed less than a hundred pounds. She stopped eating. The next time I visited Mom and Dad, I was shocked at what I saw.

This was not my mom. I had no idea that she had gone off the deep end, on a hunger strike and neither did she. She could only eat a couple of bites of food at each meal. She was suffering from decades of abuse and the loss of her beloved first-born son who was born on her birthday. She was always the strong one that held the family together. She just didn't have the strength to hold it together any longer. She kept all her emotions inside. Her insides fell apart. She had an emotional breakdown that lasted about a year. When Dad started getting better, so did she.

After the hunger strike ended, Mom convinced Dad to start seeing a psychiatrist. They went together as a couple and individually. The psychiatrist diagnosed Dad with PTSD and bipolar disorder. After researching the symptoms of bipolar, the diagnosis fit Dad in every category. Bipolar disorder, formerly called manic depression, is a mental health condition that causes extreme mood swings that include emotional highs (mania or hypomania) and lows (depression). Left untreated, bipolar disorder can result in serious problems like drug and alcohol addiction, suicide or suicide attempts, domestic violence, and many more problems that our family experienced throughout the years.

There's no sure way to prevent bipolar disorder. However, I learned that getting treatment at the earliest sign of a mental health disorder can help prevent bipolar disorder conditions from worsening.

In the back of my mind I always worried that Dad would kill Mom then himself. I worried that I would get a phone call that both my parents were dead. Dad was a sleepwalker but not a calm one. He threw TV's through walls while sleepwalking while fighting the "gooks." He was capable of taking his loaded shotgun and blowing my mother away. When I visited, I locked the spare bedroom door but knew that I wouldn't be able to avoid a blast if he pulled the trigger, and neither would Mom.

The psychiatrist prescribed Dad a drug called Abilify. Aripiprazole, sold under the brand name Abilify among others, is an atypical antipsychotic. It is recommended and primarily used in the treatment of schizophrenia and bipolar disorder. The drug was only approved by the FDA in 2004. About a month after Dad started taking Abilify his behavior started changing. I was able to have adult conversations with him. Before, conversations with Dad were on the scale of eighth grade boy jokes or he became disengaged or combative.

Abilify didn't fix all Dads problems but it put him more in the center than at the extremes of his emotions. He still had episodes of nightmares while trying to sleep. He believed that he was fighting the "gooks" in North Korea. He continued to jump out of bed and punch holes in the walls when he didn't tie his legs to the robe that hung from the ceiling.

For decades Mom tried to get help for Dad through the Veteran's Administration by assisting him with claiming PTSD as a result of trauma in the Korean War. Dad said that his ship was under attack, something exploded, he was knocked into a porthole, and he landed on his head and was unconscious for a while. That was how he remembered what happened. The war gave him a lifetime of nightmares. The Veteran's Administration always denied his claim because they didn't have any records of his ship being under attack and he didn't have medical proof that tied the PTSD to the Korean War. When he went to the disability hearings, he would tell the VA doctor that there wasn't anything wrong with him.

For those decades of Dad not being medically diagnosed with bipolar disorder and PTSD, we all suffered. Taking a pill didn't cure all his problems, but it helped. Dad and Mom went to weekly psychiatric sessions and it kept him mostly at bay.

Occasionally, he would do crazy things like when he snuck to the bank, drew out their little savings, and bought a motorcycle with the savings and financed the rest without Mom knowing about it.

Before he took got home with the motorcycle, he ripped it up and down I75 near Sun City Center gunning the accelerator as fast as it could go, like at the dirt race track forty years earlier trying to kill himself. Then, he went home and bragged to Mom that he bought a motorcycle and got it up to 125 mph. He said he could prove how fast it goes. Of course, she just about had a heart attack. He enjoyed getting a rise out of her.

She made him take the motorcycle back. She called the dealership telling them that he was on his way to return the motorcycle. After speaking with several people up the chain to the general manager, she told them that they sold a motorcycle to a crazy person who can't legally sign a contract and if he wrecked the bike, she would own the dealership. They took the revved-up motorcycle back but not without a lot of pushback. Mom gave even stronger threats of law suits.

After the motorcycle purchase, Mom took their small savings and purchased a Certificate of Deposit. She told Dad that it was drawing interest and couldn't be cashed until its expiration date or they would lose money. The expiration date always had a moving target and never seemed to expire.

Dad got a gall bladder infection that wouldn't heal. He suffered with large gallstones that required surgical removal of his gallbladder. Mom took him to the emergency room. They sat there for hours. Dad didn't like being ignored. He scooted to the middle of the floor, laid on his back like a turned over cockroach with his feet and arms flailing in the air like he was having a heart attack. Then, the medical staff took him to the back immediately.

After the surgery, he boasted that he was full of gangrene, died on the operating table, and brought back to life by the surgeon, not just once but two times. Late that night after the surgery in the hospital, he yanked out all the IV's from his arm and tried to sneak out the front door of the hospital in his robe exposing his bare ass to anyone awake.

Luckily, someone finally caught him going down the sidewalk in front of the hospital. He said that he was going to get fresh glazed donuts at Walmart. Walmart was four miles away.

Days later he told Mom that his hospital roommate was a homosexual and the roommate was trying to have sex with him in the hospital room and he had to get out of there. He didn't have a roommate. He was on powerful drugs that were adversely interacting with his psychotic medication.

Dad called my first cousin David every week or two. Dad loved to tell stories. He told David that after his gall bladder was removed the doctor gave him a bunch of pills to take to ease the pain and not get an infection.

Dad said, "Now David, I kept tryin' to swaller this big slimy pill and it jus' won't go down. I said Carol what kinda pill is it that won't swaller? Carol looked on the bottle and said the pill was a morphine suppository. I was supposed ta stick this pill up my ass not swaller it."

* * *

Dad began to lose his memory and was diagnosed with Alzheimer's and dementia. He wanted to go "home" to Kentucky and visit relatives.

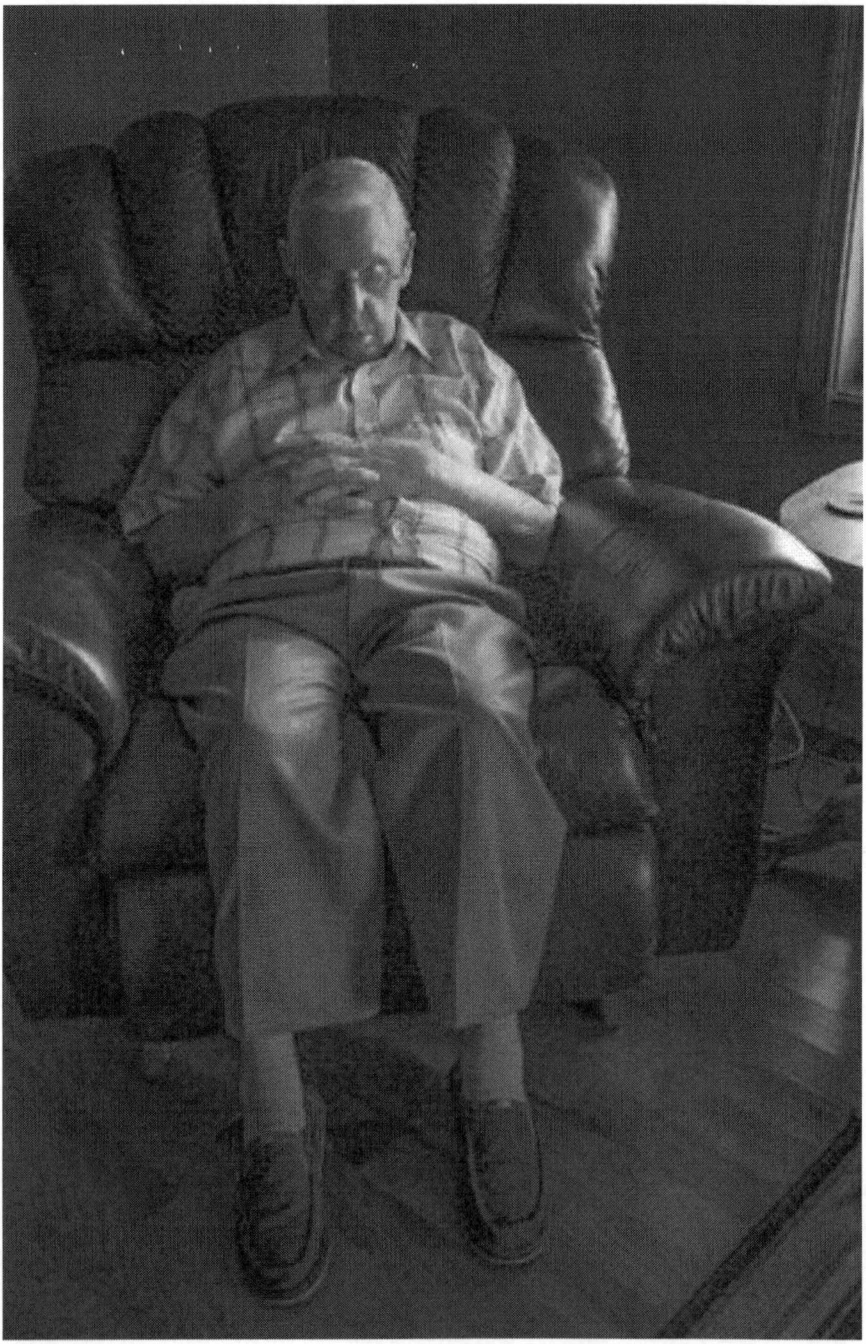

In June 2012, Mom and Dad flew into Atlanta's Hartsfield International airport. A nice gentleman from Delta strolled them both in wheelchairs through the airport's chaos. I picked them up and we drove to Greenup. Once again, we navigated Hillbilly Highway stopping at Dad's favorite Cracker Barrel restaurant. Only this time it was the last trip 'home' for Dad while he was still alive. I filmed the adventure and called the video "Kentucky Road Trip."

Mom and Dad planned for us to stay at one of my cousin's that lives close to the Darnell Cemetery where Dad's father is buried. My cousin Scotty and his wife live in a nice four-bedroom house. When it was time to go to bed, I learned that their daughter was home on break from college. Dad needed his own room to sleep. That meant I had to sleep in the same bed as Mom. I couldn't even believe it. She snored all night. I got a hotel the next morning. I should have known better. When you go "Home" it's considered rude to sleep in a hotel when there is a couch or back porch to sleep on somewhere. Rudeness trumped staying awake all night.

We visited my great aunt Dovy, sister of my great grandmother Hannah. She proudly escorted me around her house showing me all the things that belonged to my great grandmother. The house was full of her antique belongings. Throughout my life Dad mentioned that he didn't get a single thing to remind him of his beloved grandmother. I shot a few images of Hannah and Henry hanging on the wall.

I don't know how Hannah's final estate was concluded but I felt Dad's abandonment. My great aunt didn't live in great granny's house but she inherited a lot of her belongings. My heart was heavy with sadness as he walked around seeing all his grandmother's possessions that he grew up with. We drove back to Sun City Center. I felt that Dad knew he wouldn't be going back home again.

* * *

Mom and Dad entered Walmart in the entrance by the produce. Each parent would secure a handicap cart and go their own ways with agreed upon instructions to meet at the door where they come in when finished shopping.

Dad navigated through Walmart with his cane sticking out the side of the shopping cart basket and clueless to the many clothes racks that his cane grabbed and knocked to the floor as he drove by. Everything else in his way also tumbled to the ground. When I witnessed the merchandise taking a dive, I positioned the cane to lean out the rear of the metal basket. The cane sat too close to the steering wheel so he put it back where it originated, pressed the power lever and took off like a bat out of hell. He didn't care that all that crap was taking a nose dive. He was on a mission. I just went to the front of the store and waited for both of them to show up to leave. It made me a nervous wreck watching him single handedly dismantle Walmart.

Mom and I would just wait and wait at the entrance that we came into. When I asked what was taking him so long to get his Pepsi and donuts, Mom said, "I don't know." She wouldn't buy the sugar products for him. He had to have it. His sole purpose of going to Walmart was to get a twelve pack of Pepsi and a box of stale glazed donuts.

After speed searching through the store several times, I discovered that he was at the other entrance. He sat outside in the road of the heavily trafficked parking lot in the electric Walmart handicap cart while cars zipped around him. He was waiting to be picked up.

This uncanny excitement was typical during their daily adventures anytime they left the house. One time he went to Walmart by himself, got lost and couldn't find his way home. He didn't go by himself again. But mostly, we enjoyed a couple of fairly good years with 'good Dennis' before he passed on October 29, 2014.

The final events that led to Dad's death were horribly painful for him and for our family. He suffered enormous pain with his back from the fall decades previous and the unsuccessful surgeries to make it better. He could barely walk with tiny shuffled steps holding on tight with a walker. The pain killers only went so far.

Dad was also diagnosed with Parkinson's disease. He got to the point where he couldn't take care of himself and Mom was hanging on by a thread taking care of him.

On September 10, 2014, Dad began to hallucinate and see bugs crawling everywhere that weren't there. He started becoming irritated and aggressive. He hit Mom and fell to the floor when he swung at her the second time but she had backed away. He couldn't get back up off the floor. She called Dan for help.

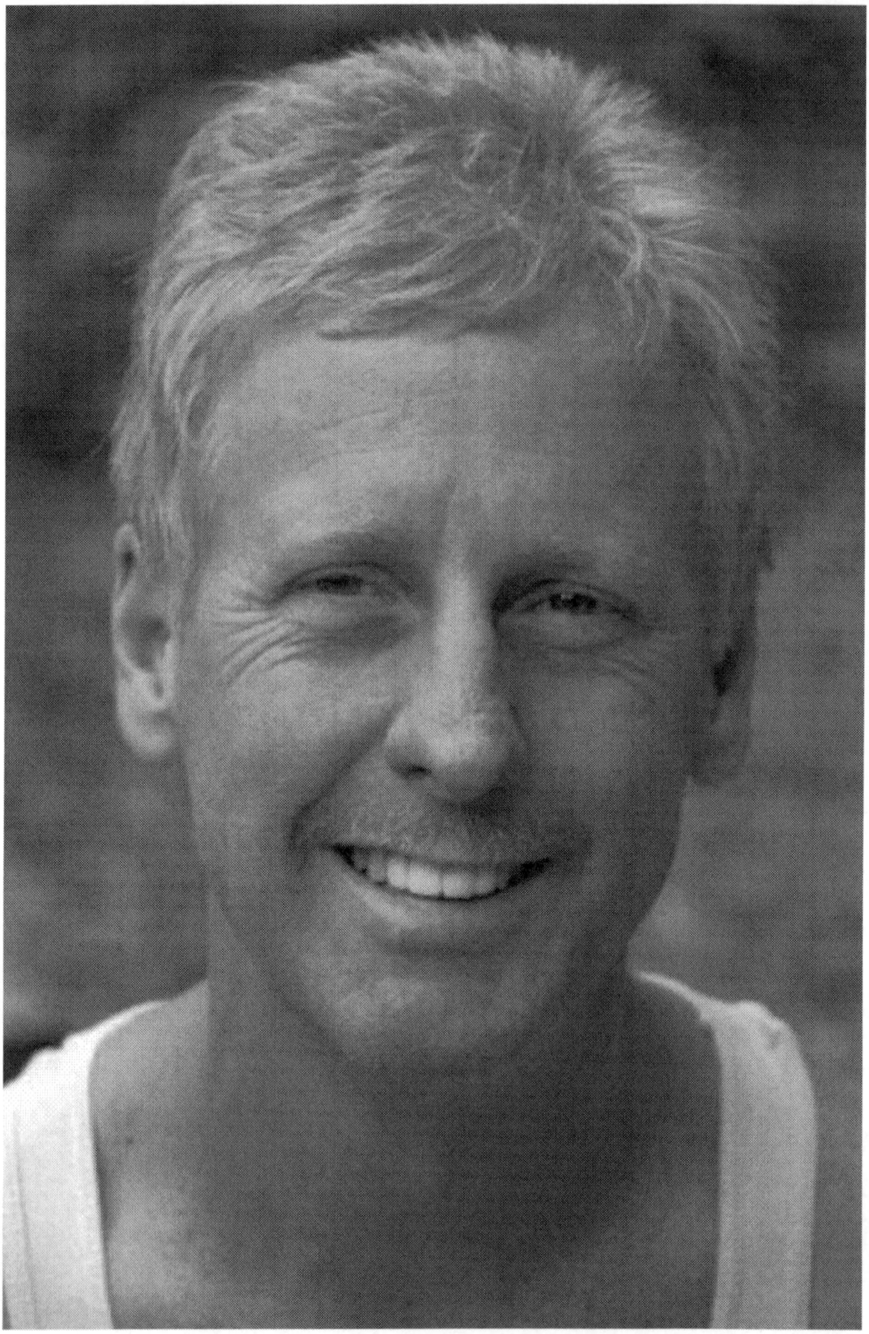

Dan had become a hardworking, strong, and determined man. He lives about thirty miles from Sun City Center in a town called Dover. Dan worked for Hillsborough County as machine operator for thirty years until he recently retired. He was the one who lived closest to Mom and Dad and kept an eye on them. He told Dad that he needed to make a choice of either going to jail or to the hospital. Dan called 911, an ambulance came, strapped Dad to a stretcher and took him away to the psychiatric ward of the local hospital. Dan had to Baker Act Dad for his violent behavior. That was the last time Dad was home alive.

After the first day in the hospital the staff wanted to release him to go home instead of to a rehabilitation facility. They said that he didn't have a condition that qualified him for rehabilitation. We applied for him to go to several skilled nursing facilities, but they all turned him down because he didn't have a long-term care plan. How does anyone have a long-term plan that doesn't have any money?

We decided that it was not safe for him to go back home, not for him and not for Mom. She could no longer take care of him. When he fell, he couldn't get up and she didn't have the strength to lift a 230-pound body off the floor. He couldn't go to the bathroom by himself and wore a diaper. And, he had just hit her. He wasn't going back home to do that again.

A really nice nurse at the hospital helped us navigate the medical nightmare system. When Dad started aspirating the next day, he became qualified to go into Hospice care because of the new "symptom." Square pegs had to fit into the square holes. His food and water didn't go into his stomach, but into his lungs so he was taken to Hospice.

While in Hospice the staff was not allowed to administer Dad's psychotic medication. In fact, they refused to let Mom bring it in for him to take. He started going through serious withdraws without the Abilify. Again, he pulled all the IV's out of his arms and tried to escape. He wanted to go home. When he stood up and tried to walk, he fell like a plank straight forward into the tiled floor smashing all the teeth out of his mouth. He was a complete mess.

The staff at Hospice tried everything they could to make Mom take Dad back to the house. We insisted that it was not safe for him to go there. Hospice told us that Dad was not dying quickly enough and could not stay in Hospice more than five days. They threatened Mom, then me with putting Dad in an ambulance and dropping him off at the front door. They told us that she had better be home to let him in the house.

When Hospice called me at work in Atlanta and told me they were literally going to drop Dad on the front porch in an hour, I threatened them with a lawsuit if they attempted that maneuver. They told me that he needed to go to a skilled nursing facility, that they couldn't manage his symptoms. The nurse said that he needed a thickening agent in his food and liquids for hydration. They weren't allowed to do that in Hospice. No skilled nursing facility would take him with his psychiatric problems.

It was clear in Dad's living will to not apply life-sustaining procedures to his body, not even nourishment and hydration so he could be permitted to die. He kept whispering between shallow gurgling breaths that he wanted to die. He was ready to go home to the Lord.

Dad was on so many medications that it was hard for Mom to keep track of what he needed to take and how much of it when he was home. When Dad entered hospice, Mom gave the head nurse a list of his medications and they verified the list with Medicare. He took medication for PSTD, Parkinson's Disease, Alzheimer's, dementia, pain, arthritis, high cholesterol, cardiovascular disease, stomach acid, liquid to make you crap, and pills to stop the crapping.

I found out that reason Hospice wouldn't give Dad the Abilify was because it costs too much money. Medicare wouldn't pay for it while he was in Hospice. Mom brought the Abilify from home and demanded that Hospice give it to him. He finally got relief from horrific hallucinations after it got back into his system.

Based on our experience with Hospice, it was all about the money. The case manager told me that the rules changed for Medicare. Once Dad's symptoms became manageable, Medicare would not pay for Hospice. Hospice demanded that Mom pay for the cost of his care. She didn't have a pot to piss in. They didn't have savings or a plan. And his conditions didn't get better.

It was a three-ring circus managing Dad's care at Hospice. Nobody wanted Dad. Once he hit the floor and busted all his teeth out, Hospice was afraid that we would sue them. We didn't. We just wanted him to be safe and at peace. That never happened. He was a hot potato. They made it a mission to try to get rid of him. He was too much work. We were told that they couldn't babysit him to make sure he didn't get up again and fall. Laws prevented him from being restrained. They wanted easy deaths and Dad didn't fit that bill.

Every day at work I got phone calls from Hospice threatening me to take him out of there. I'm sorry he was so hard to take care of. He has been difficult his whole life. Why would it be any different on his death bed? How could they expect Mom to take care of him when they couldn't or didn't want to as trained professionals? It was a catch twenty-two. He was barely over the income level to qualify for a free skilled nursing home from the government with his Social Security income. The nurses made it their full-time job to get him placed in one. Nobody would take Dad. Hospice wanted to abandon Dad but were stuck with him.

Dad died a month after entering Hospice. He could no longer swallow. The radiation treatments from the cancer caused his throat to swell shut. He starved to death. A couple weeks before passing the preacher came to see Dad and asked if he needed anything. Dad said, "Dolly Parton" and laughed.

Dad mentioned the very young girl at the end of his bed wearing a dress. There wasn't a young girl in the room. Who was this angel? He mentioned her before, years ago. He needed an angel, one that would have mercy on his tortured soul.

I told Mom not to worry. We'll all be together again someday, God willing. In Dad's dying days, he never said that he was sorry. He never acted like he ever did anything wrong. He never had before. Dad didn't talk about his feelings. Men of that generation just didn't. I knew that he loved me and was proud of my accomplishments without him saying a word. He wasn't mentally capable of expressing sorrow for his bad behavior. Empathy wasn't part of his DNA. At least that's what I choose to believe. He suffered deep depressions after episodes of being violent. I could tell that he was remorseful, but not enough to stop, not without the right medication.

After Dad was cremated, I divided his ashes in half. When the two-hundred-and-thirty-pound military headstone arrived at Mom's front door in Sun City Center, my brother Dan loaded the headstone into Mom's oil leaking old Cadillac and drove "Bad Dennis" to the Darnell Cemetery way out in Load, Kentucky in Greenup County. Dad wanted to be buried next to his father. "Good Dennis" rests in the other urn in Mom's closet next to the Electrolux, at least for now. Dad went home. God rest his soul.

19

Passion

I love taking pictures. Dad let me use his camera growing up until I purchased my own cameras in the military. I have taken pictures all my life but was never formally educated in photography.

Beginning in 2005, I studied photography by taking all the adult education classes that the Showcase School of Photography in Atlanta had to offer. I gained confidence and started showing my images at the Atlanta Photography Group's monthly critiques. The photographers in the group provided critical feedback and helped me compose and print images at a professional level.

After taking tons of individual images, I was ready to start a photography project. In 1998 my wife Julie and I purchased a small brick ranch in a neighborhood along Cheshire Bridge Road in Atlanta, Georgia. She suggested that I photograph our neighborhood community. The one-mile road is locally known as Atlanta's Red-Light District because of its many strip clubs, gay bars, and adult novelty stores. There are also multiple locally owned restaurants and small businesses along this infamous road.

Initially, I walked up and down Cheshire Bridge Road with my camera to get exercise and to relive the stress of the work day that included a congested traffic commute. In the beginning I only took pictures of the outside of the shacks and buildings that were (and still are) being torn down and gentrified. I tried to go inside to take pictures but was told "no" everywhere I went. I wanted to capture the lives of people in their environment but first I had to earn their trust.

I kept going inside strip clubs, drag clubs, bars, restaurants, and many seedy places. I was certainly not unfamiliar with these establishments from a life of trying to coax my dad out of trashy bars as a child growing up. I started up conversations with anyone that would listen to me about how I wanted to bring awareness of our special community to others by creating a book of photographs of the people and places on Cheshire Bridge Road.

I began to get past the gatekeepers and into the offices of owners and managers so I could take pictures inside the clubs. Once I got permission, then I needed to build trust with the performers. I took many pictures of performers on stage. After I got home and processed the images, I would make prints and go back to find them to give them their pictures. They loved the prints.

I was shooting stage performance pictures at The Jungle (drag club) one Saturday night when I got the courage to go behind the stage and attempt to take pictures of the performers getting ready for their show. I was a nervous wreck. This was a BIG NO NO. I needed to be creative. I could see the drag queens getting ready behind a big black curtain.

I poked my camera through the curtain. I saw Biqtch Puddin' looking to see what was going on. In a dramatic way I jumped out from behind the curtains and loudly announced that I was there to take pictures while pointing my camera in every direction. Biqtch Puddin' laughed and said, "Well alright then." Biqtch Puddin' graduated from Savannah College of Art and Design (SCAD) and has gone on to make a big name for herself in California as a drag super monster in the TV series Dracula. Biqtch Puddin' gave me a break that spread through the drag community.

Taking pictures was about creating a connection in my community. I found each journey traversing the road insightful. I sought Moments when people were between the ordinary and extraordinary, the down and the out, the up and the coming. I strived to see inside people to show the outside world their humanity. By doing that, I was also showing my own humanity. I photographed this strip so my viewers could absorb and expand their own horizons and understandings of a world that may be unfamiliar to them.

I am passionate about humanity and documenting the diversity that exists within our world. And, it all began from my experience growing up in a home full of adversity.

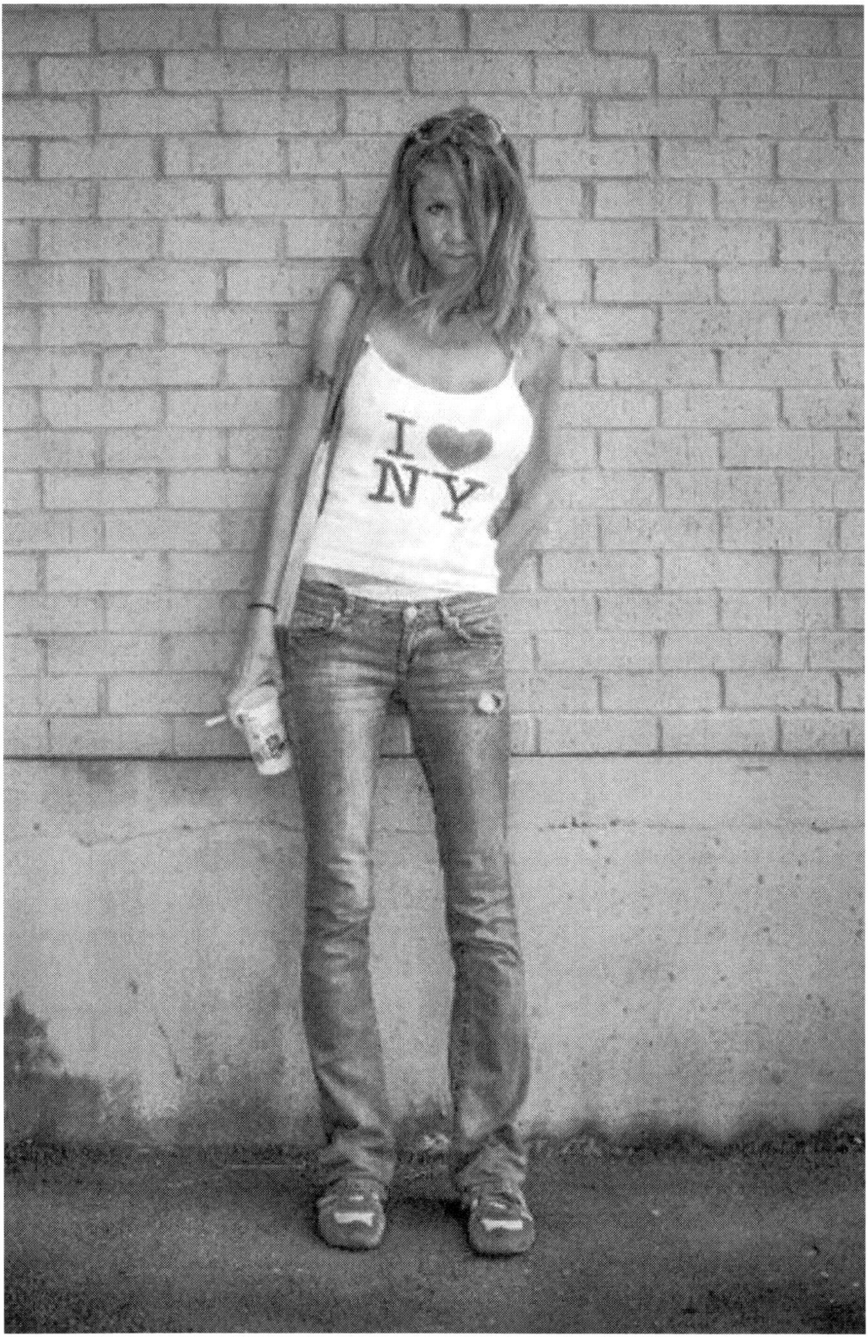
I
NY

I took a picture of a woman I call "I Heart NY" behind the Old Ace Hardware store on Cheshire Bridge Road. When I saw this apparently beaten woman, I knew immediately that she was a drug addict and was prostituting for her next hit. I felt the sadness in her heart. I told her how beautiful her eyes were and that she had really pretty hair. She bared her soul in the picture. I cried all the way home and still cry when I see this image. This brave capture kept me photographing Cheshire Bridge Road for a decade. The I Heart NY woman could have been me if I had chosen a path of destruction or continued to feel sorry for myself while in high school and beyond.

I took a couple hundred thousand images along Cheshire Bridge Road. In 2018, curator Randy Gue at the Stuart A. Rose Manuscript, Archives and Rare Book Library (MARBL) at Emory University acquired the Cheshire Bride Road collection of images for historical archival and research purposes. The people and places that I took pictures of on Cheshire Bridge Road now have a home. I couldn't be more honored to have Emory University as the steward of this collection.

Randy Gue and Atlanta aid's activist Jesse Peel believed this body of work deserved to be preserved. If it wasn't for them, it may have never happened. Many of my images have also been displayed in various parts of the world such as Beijing, China; Berlin, Germany; New York City; and Tbilisi, Capital of Georgia.

I invite you to view some of my favorite images on my website at www.teridarnell.com.

* * *

About every five years I landed different position at UPS' headquarters in Atlanta because I needed a new challenge. Throughout the years, in conference meetings we'd go around the room sharing ideas. More than not, my ideas would be dismissed. Then, a light would go off in one of the men's head. When it was their turn to speak, they would say the same thing with a different spin, only then was the idea heard and implemented. It was deemed brilliant and he was congratulated and often promoted. Master men spinners took many women's ideas and made them their own. If you made waves you could be out of a job. I learned how to keep my mouth shut just like I did with the domestic violence that continuously penetrated our household growing up with Dad being in control and anyone who questioned this authority got punished. I kept silent.

Despite the roadblocks of male dominance at UPS and at home with my rearing, I became successful. My work commanded respect and couldn't be ignored. I was rated in the top ten percent of my peer group over and over and over again, for my entire career. If the goal was 100% for the annual rating, my team always achieved a higher percent. But I still didn't get the promotions like my peers with less of a rating.

I was told many times that I needed a "Godfather" who could take me up the ladder. But like high school, the men weren't attracted to me. I was too much like them and that's not fashionable for getting promoted. I was told by a women District Manager (there were very few women in upper management) that I needed to act more like the men's mother or their best friend, not as a competitor and needed to be really likeable in their eyes. Everyone liked me, I didn't understand. It wasn't in my DNA to act like a mother. Was "Likeable" code for sleeping with them? That wasn't about to happen.

In the meantime, I created a new subgroup in my department with innovative programs for UPS that took the company from delivering paper-based training to developing programs using multi-media similar to television commercials with quick hits for the sales force. I wrote compelling scripts and filmed the President of Sales providing messages to the global sales force almost on the fly. It would have taken weeks to hire an outside company to do this work and many thousands of dollars. My team could get her messages out in a matter of a couple of days.

The program was a huge success for UPS. I created this program without the help of the company. I used all of my own camera equipment for two years until I told them that I was no longer going to use my personal equipment for UPS business. I had to use my equipment to get the program started, to prove that it would be successful.

I asked my boss what would happen if someone knocked over my $4,000 camera. He said that UPS wouldn't pay for it. That's when I protested and got my budget approved to purchase the equipment needed to run a small multi-media group. Previously, my budget was denied for two years.

I was praised with many 'Atta-girls' for my innovation and creativity, but received little pay raises that didn't cover inflation and no opportunity for a promotion. I saw the writing on the wall years before when I kept getting passed up for promotions. It didn't stop me from trying my hardest and giving my best.

When I retired from UPS, I was asked by our department president to give a speech in the auditorium about my experiences in front of two hundred people. Most people tell funny stories that happened during their career like the fat driver who ate his way through his delivery route. Of course, I couldn't do that. I had to take it one step farther.

I wanted the speech to my peers to be about diversity, humanity and inclusivity. These fundamental characteristics weren't always present at UPS. Often in my career it was about exclusion of people who were different, like me. I was a single woman without kids in an environment of white married men with kids. That alone separated me from most of my peers. As time went on, the demographics changed but the management team remained largely white male at the corporate office.

For instance, on my first day of work at UPS' corporate headquarters in Atlanta, I walked down the long-wooded cement path from the multi-tiered parking lot so beautifully tucked away in the woods. I traveled alongside the seven-story glittering new glass building until I got to the security entrance. As I approached the door I looked up and witnessed a sea of starched white shirts inside the enormous cafeteria.

The cafeteria was full of all white men as far as I could see. They glowed like sea gulls at the beach snatching pieces of bread thrown by tourists. The sea gulls were everywhere. I questioned my decision of working there where diversity seemed non-existent. I wondered what I got myself into. That Moment I knew it would be a career with many uphill battles, and it was. I was up for the challenge. It was worth every bit of it. UPS and I grew together.

For my retirement speech I gathered appropriate and thoughtful images from my Cheshire Bridge Road collection and put together a slide show to tell stories about diversity, inclusion, humanity, and perseverance. Essentially, I told the story of my own life's perils but through the images of others, their stories, and my brief encounters with the people along the way.

The morning of the speech, I provided a thumb drive of the slideshow to the department meeting committee leader. I already had the images approved by our department president. He knew the story and supported my creativity.

The up and coming millennial leader came to the seventh floor and stepped inside my seven by seven-foot cubicle that was home for twenty years. He told me that I couldn't show these images, that the "committee" deemed them inappropriate. He told me that the images would have to be approved by the legal department and that could take weeks. It was my last day in the office. He set my red turning white hair on fire.

For the first time in my career, my red-headed temper came barreling down between his eyes as I fired out that I wasn't giving a speech unless it was with those images. We high-stepped it to President's office. I had been his speech writer for more than a year and was on great terms with the big boss. He said there wasn't a problem with my images or speech and that was that. The fumes that blew out my ears and had my hair standing straight up on its ends began to extinguish.

I was given a standing ovation after the speech. I hopefully accomplished opening the sea for all to see a world different than their own by telling stories and showing images unlike any showed before at UPS. I remain hopeful that I helped others be more accepting of people not just like themselves.

The bright new leader quickly came by to apologize after the speech. I could tell that his eyes and heart widened. As with the rest of the "committee," they only wanted to see and do what they already understood. I believe the leader will remember that day when he runs the company in some capacity years from now.

I hope that he and others will offer a future to people who aren't just like them, like Nancy Frank (who hired me at UPS) did for me. If each of us would find a few diamonds to polish our communities will grow rich with love and kindness instead of growing more divisiveness.

UPS offered me the beginning of a new life that lasted twenty-five years. Nothing about it was easy, but I kept shifting gears forward with an occasional setback. The company provided me with a plan to achieve financial freedom so I could retire earlier than I had ever imagined when I accepted the job at age twenty-nine.

20

Peace

Over twenty years ago Mom stopped trying to make friends. It was a full-time job taking care of Dad and the house. If anyone showed interest in becoming friends, he would run them off.

After Dad passed, she was interested in joining the Kentucky Club in Sun City Center. You name it and the retirement community has a club for it.

I encouraged Mom to attend the Kentucky Club luncheon at a local restaurant to meet new people. She hoped the Kentucky Club would share her interests. Mom loves watching the Kentucky Wildcats play basketball on TV, both men and women's teams. She wears their college T-shirts and shorts for good luck during a game.

She has the game schedule posted on her bedroom door. Mom doesn't miss a game. She knows all the names of the players and their statistics. She's a true diehard fan of college basketball when Wildcats play ball.

I could tell Mom was nervous about going to the luncheon. She's not one to put herself out there. She thought about wearing her Kentucky Wildcat T-Shirt but instead chose one of the pretty outfits that she bought from Nearly New, her favorite place to shop, a second-hand store in Sun City Center.

In fact, for the last twenty years she hasn't bought clothes from anywhere else except for Walmart underwear. Every time she finds a new white Alfred Dunner pull over cotton top from Nearly New, she shakes it in my face and says, "One dollar, this would be fifty dollars at the mall! It still has the tags on it." She's so proud of her treasure hunt finds. She has at least forty white tops from Nearly New. Once I counted them.

This time she put on a fancier top with matching pants then made her way to the luncheon. Mom found three couples from Louisville, Kentucky sitting at a table in the restaurant. As a widower she was the odd woman out.

Louisville's the largest city in Kentucky and known for The Kentucky Derby horse racing event. Writer Jesse Stuart grew up in Greenup, their honorary claim to fame. Mom didn't fit in with the city slickers. The men chatted about Republican politics while the wives listened intently dangling their diamond bracelets. She didn't go back to another luncheon.

Mom makes her errand rounds through Sun City Center as she did before Dad's death. Dad was her lifelong project. He left her with nothing but an oil leaking Cadillac and a mortgage to pay for using her below poverty level Social Security income. She manages to make it work.

Now she sits at home alone in peace for the first time in her life, but not always. I call every evening to ask what she's been up to all day. She says, "I don't know, but it took me all day to do it."

Her family visits often. She loves those grand and great grand-babies, and all her family. It's always been about her family, never about herself. Mostly, she reads every book in the library, just like she taught me to read, learn, study, understand, love, give, live, and forgive.

* * *

Mostly I drive to visit Mom. Sometimes I fly. On a recent trip, on my ride back to the Tampa International Airport I met Lyft driver Laura. Forty-four-year-old Laura was raised in New Jersey. She served in the United States Navy in Charleston. The Navy wanted to reassign her to Guantanamo Bay Cuba. She was a single mother and wouldn't be allowed to take her two young daughters on the deployment.

According to Laura, the Navy suggested that she leave the kids with relatives for two years. She didn't have any relatives willing to take on that responsibility. Her commanding officer said that he would take them like they were house pets that could be left with anyone to care for them. Laura couldn't abandon her young children so the Navy discharged her with a hardship dismissal. She loved the Navy and wanted to make a career out of it.

When Laura was seventeen, she met her future husband. After they were married the beatings began. After the first time he promised it would never happen again. He was an angry man and would explode if she dropped a lid in the kitchen. She loved him more than the pain of the beatings.

He left no marks by punching her temples from side-to-side like a punching bag. She got pregnant. He pushed her down the stairs with the baby inside her. She left him and moved back into her mother's house who knew nothing about the abuse at first because she was afraid to tell anyone. After giving birth to her daughter she thought her husband could change. He promised to be a better man and a good father. She wanted to believe him. She wanted them all to be a family. She went back to him.

The beatings became worse. The two-year-old daughter was always crying, agitated, and nervous. Laura worried so much about her daughter that she left her husband and joined the Navy. Her only hope was to have a better life for her child.

I noticed the disability sticker in the tiny car when she picked me up for a ride to the airport. Laura mentioned that she has permanent brain injury from many concussions where her husband beat her head in.

She said that she was called for jury duty the following week and couldn't understand why she had to serve after providing a doctor's letter stating her disability. She said that she can't remember many events from her past. She said that she can't perform most jobs because she forgets instructions seconds after told. But she said that she can drive with no problem. She follows the map on her phone app.

She stayed in the right lane at a steady methodical and calculated speed as cars weaved in and out of traffic. I felt safe and secure.

It was a one-hour drive to the airport, an hour that I connected with her old soul and understood more about why Mom can't remember events of the past. It's not selective memory but her brain cells were beaten out of her memory forever. Some memories lost are for the good, and others can't fill her heart with joy because they are gone and will never come back.

* * *

Mom and I usually play gin rummy. Whoever wins two out of three games is the grand champion and gets to boast to anyone that will listen. Mom's hard to beat in a game of cards. She's a fierce competitor. Over the years I picked up on her strategy so we always have a challenging match.

During yesterday's first of a possible three games when it was my turn to deal, at least five times when I cut the cards the ace of spades showed up on the bottom of the deck. During one shuffle the ace of spades flew out of the deck and landed face up on the table. We both laughed out loud simultaneously, nervously. The ace of spades symbolizes death.

The next day after I arrived home in the daylight and an owl flew in front of me as I was walking around the block, another sign of death. The next day my aunt Bernice in Kentucky passed away. I had planned to be up there in two weeks to see her. It's been a few years since I've been back to Greenup. But Greenup is not my home any longer. My happy and supportive home has been with my wife Julie in Atlanta for the last twenty-one years.

Afterword

Typically, abusers become violent or hurtful out of their merciless desire to be in control. It can be challenging for their loved ones to fully realize what's happening to them when while in survival mode. The abused are afraid to leave and often lack financial resources to support themselves. Many don't have a supporting extended family willing to intervene.

Statistics indicate that on average nearly twenty people per minute are physically abused by an intimate partner in the United States alone. This abuse happens to more than ten million women and men a year in the U.S. Look around. Chances are you know someone being abused this is keeping silent.

Over one third of women become victims of physical violence by an intimate partner during their lifetime. Over seventy percent of all murder-suicides involve an intimate partner and over ninety percent of these victims are female. And, many innocent children witness intimate partner violence each year. These numbers should be zero.

If parents can learn and understand that their behavior is manifested inside their own children, then maybe they will be better protectors of the children's mental health. But it takes a village to help, a community to provide support. This support doesn't come from the government. This support comes from family members, teachers, church members, co-workers, bosses, friends, neighbors, and anyone else willing to get involved. If I didn't have these channels of guidance and support throughout my life, I would have become part of the downward spiral of society.

Children need role models and mentors throughout their lives to help them become fully capable human beings. I was fortunate to have both wonderful male and female mentors in the military, at church, and through friends and colleagues.

Mom and Dad understood the importance of having a "village". We visited "home" so we could bond with our granny, aunts, uncles, and cousins in hopes creating a lasting tribe and a place to call home with unconditional love, something Dad didn't experience growing up.

While writing this story, I saw a T-shirt in Portland, Oregon at the PDX airport from Ann Arbor T-Shirt Company® that had a small camper trailer on the front. On the back it read, "Mess with Me, Mess with the Whole Trailer Park." When a child is surrounded by loving, caring, smart, wise, guiding adults, they can be free to try, fail, get back up, and try even harder because they know that their "trailer park" is behind them. That "trailer park" can be you, their relatives, teachers, social workers, church, sports teams, coaches, neighbors, clubs, and groups that are willing to show interest in the child and have their back when things go wrong and they can't protect themselves.

Maybe you can help provide an environment for children to prosper. Every smile and positive encouragement will make a difference. Positive reinforcement helps negate the negative responses that children are exposed to. Help them love themselves and they will show the same love to others.

If you're already successful in your own life, you can provide opportunities for someone else to reach their capacity too. For girls and women, the doors don't open as easily as the ones for men. Sometimes we just need a crack to see light. Be the one who sheds the light. Find that diamond in the rough and polish her. For that gift of love and kindness, she will polish a diamond too. Keep shifting gears forward. Find your rhythm. Don't quit. Don't give up.

We don't know what goes on in other people's homes and that makes it harder to help, but if it's your home and you or your children are experiencing abuse, it's time to break the silence and stop the violence. Granny would say, "Shit or get off the pot."

About the Author

Teri Darnell, intrepid daughter of a hillbilly father and descendant of a long line of unflinchingly resilient Appalachian women, springs from a life of violence and uncertainty to one of self-made happiness by way of the Air Force, corporate success and a talent for capturing truth with her photography.

Teri is a graduate of Baldwin Wallace University with an Executive MBA and The University of Maryland with a Bachelor's degree in Business Management.

www.teridarnell.com

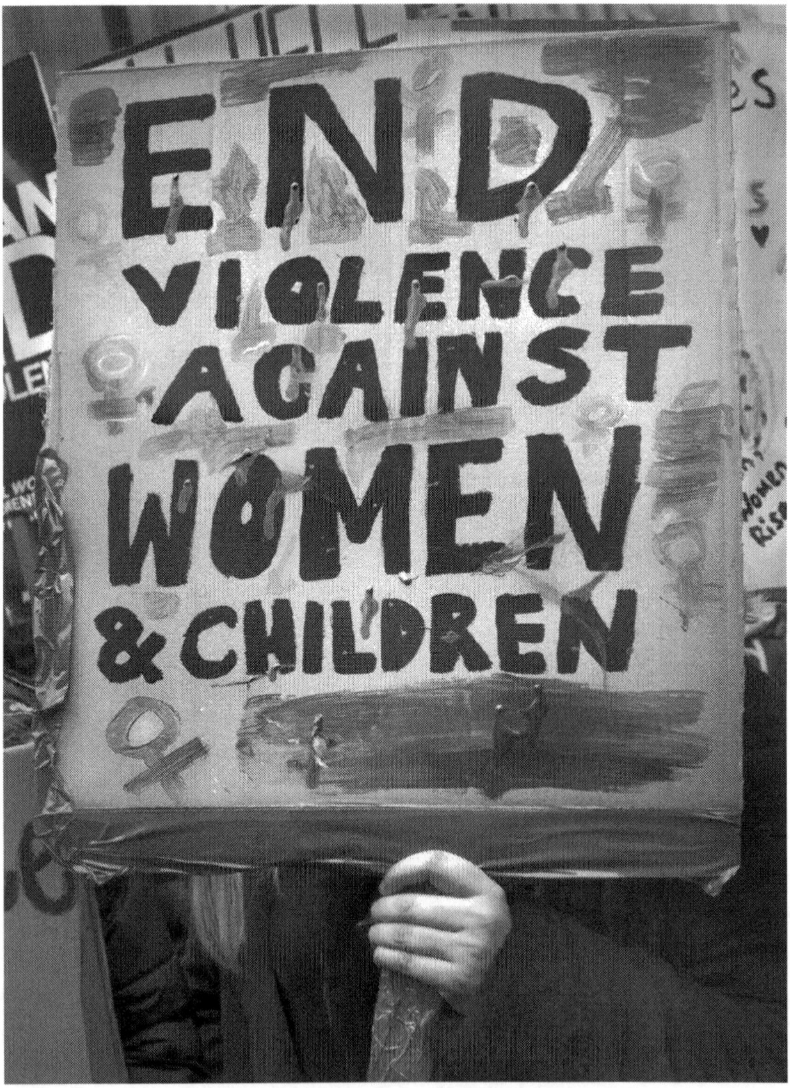
END
VIOLENCE
AGAINST
WOMEN
& CHILDREN

Made in the USA
Columbia, SC
04 February 2019